fresh from the garden *cookbook*

fresh from the garden *cookbook*

RECIPES INSPIRED BY KITCHEN GARDENS

ann lovejoy PHOTOGRAPHS BY ROBIN BACHTLER CUSHMAN

SASQUATCH BOOKS

To Peter and Andrew, Matt, Simon, and Gabriel for being so much fun to feed
To Signora Savino for teaching me to savor
To mom for teaching me to clean up as I cook!

Printed in Singapore
Published by Sasquatch Books
Distributed by Publishers Group West
12 11 10 09 08 07 06 05   6 5 4 3 2 1

Book design: Kate Basart
Photography: Robin Bachtler Cushman / Food Styling: Christy Nordstrom
Copyeditors: Rebecca Pepper, Alice Copp Smith
Indexer: Miriam Bulmer
These recipes appeared in different form in *The Seattle Post-Intelligencer*.

Library of Congress Cataloging-in-Publication Data
Lovejoy, Ann, 1951-
Fresh from the garden cookbook : recipes inspired by kitchen gardens /
Ann Lovejoy ; photographs by Robin Bachtler Cushman.
    p.   cm.
    includes index
    ISBN 1-57061-427-X
    1. Cookery, American--Pacific Northwest style.
    2. Gardening--Northwest, Pacific. I. Title.
    TX715.2.P32L68 2005
    641.59795--dc22   2004051029

SASQUATCH BOOKS
119 South Main Street, Suite 400 / Seattle, WA 98104 / (206) 467-4300
www.sasquatchbooks.com / custserv@sasquatchbooks.com

why organic?

For nearly 20 years, I have lived and gardened on a semi-rural island a short ferry ride away from Seattle. Huckleberries and fresh salmonberries fringe the edge of my backyard, and each spring, I gather native fiddlehead fronds to stir-fry with hops shoots and infant asparagus. Though I now have the luxury of sun and space to grow whatever I like, I understand that your garden may not be big enough for rows of corn and hills of beans. In my time I, too, have lived in a third floor walk-up, growing herbs and tomatoes on the fire escape and runner beans in window boxes.

For some years now, I've been writing recipes for the *Seattle Post-Intelligencer*. These food columns feature fresh, locally grown produce that could come from your own backyard or from your favorite farmers market or grocery store. Each week, I encourage readers to grow, buy, and cook with organically grown or raised foods as much as possible.

Why? Partly because organically grown food contributes to the well-being of the planet, and partly because it contributes to the well-being of

Fruits and vegetables you grow yourself using organic gardening techniques not only taste better, they're better for you.

humanity. In addition, I love really good food, and there is no better food available, both in nutritive quality and in full, rich flavor, than organically raised edibles. I offer this combination cookbook and garden book in the hope of enticing you to try cooking with and possibly growing at least a few of these delicious, wholesome, nutritious foods for yourself.

To encourage you to experiment, I've organized the recipes seasonally, adding tips on using a wide range of vegetables, greens, fruits, and herbs at their peak of freshness. Each section of the book opens with an essay that offers an overview of typical garden activities for that season, including timing and techniques for growing and harvesting many foods that grow well here in the maritime Northwest. You'll learn easy, effective organic gardening techniques like mulching with compost, which feeds the soil and lets the soil feed the plants.

At the end of each section, you'll find a Gardening Calendar for the season, listing what to plant, what to harvest, and what's to be found in local markets. Each calendar is followed by Gardening Notes for the vegetables, fruits, and herbs that are ready for harvesting in that season

Copper bowl and fountain amid lush garlic and salad greens.

ents you can't find in your own backyard, there are local resources for any and all of them, from farmers markets to our outstanding regional grocery stores, which stock fresh, organic fruits, vegetables, and herbs as a matter of course. Just to keep things simple, I suggest substitutions for anything that might prove challenging.

Weighing the costs

Once the exclusive province of health food die-hards, organically grown food has become increasingly popular over the past decade. Some studies indicate that people with food sensitivities may be reacting to pesticide residues as well as to a specific food allergen. When it comes to putting food in their children's or grandchildren's mouths, many people are rethinking old habits. Sprays that kill bugs and weeds on contact have been well demonstrated to harm humans, too. When excess herbicide and pesticide gets into water systems, whether as runoff from agriculture or just from weed-and-feed residues being washed into the nearest gutter, the toxins also affect frogs and fish, birds and bees, and all kinds of aquatic and wild life.

Human drinking water is similarly affected.

so that you can use them in the featured recipes. The Gardening Notes tell you in detail when and how to plant each ingredient, how to cultivate it, and which varieties do especially well in our region.

While these recipes may include ingredi-

A colorful mix of cabbage, chard, and dahlias.

Studies done early in this brand-new century reveal that the water supply of every major city in North America carries measurable and often dangerous levels of agricultural and manufacturing chemicals. In Washington State, every important body of water, including lakes, ponds, rivers, and streams, as well as municipal water supplies, shows contamination with more than 20 common pesticides. Even after treatment, many water supplies show measurable amounts of steroids and antibiotics in addition to pesticide residues. Human drugs of choice show up also, including caffeine and Prozac.

Not a day goes by without a new environmental horror story appearing in the news. As a result, organic food sales are soaring. For many folks, the only real stopper is price. It costs more to farm organically on a small scale, because it takes more time and effort than it does to run a chemically dependent agribusiness. On the other hand, when we take into account the true cost of growing food with toxins, the price of organic food looks a lot better. Add in the cost of cleaning up the soil and air and water, of recovering lost topsoil, of restoring lost or damaged habitat, and of protecting newly endangered species like salmon that can't tolerate agricultural toxins, and conventional farming starts to look pretty expensive.

One great way to get around the price problem is for each of us to buy as much organic produce as possible. The more we support organic farming, the better the price of organic food becomes. By supporting local farmers, as well as national companies that offer organic foods, we help them all to be more efficient and cost-effective.

Another great way to eat well at a reasonable cost is to grow at least some of your own food. Even the smallest garden has room for a barrel of herbs and salad greens. Intensive organic methods allow gardeners to feed a family of four year round from a quarter-acre of ground. Few of us have that much room, or even the time it would take to grow and store that much food, but almost all of us can grow a few tomatoes and as many fresh herbs as we can use.

If you think of organic gardening as difficult or mysterious, I have good news for you. Over the past thirty years or so (since I've been gardening organically), a lot has changed. New technology has given us effective and safe products with which we can solve almost every common garden problem without toxins. New tools and techniques

Growing organic is an easy way to stay healthy and protect the environment.

make garden preparation, plant care, and harvesting simpler. Should we choose to put food by as well as eat it fresh, advances in food storage techniques also simplify the processing stage.

Some of the most important differences in the new organic gardening are due to the way we view and therefore treat the soil. Although scientists have realized for a long time that soil is in many senses alive, only recently have we had the technology and perhaps the interest to learn just how excitingly complex and diverse soil populations can be.

Because we now know that soil can be harmed by many traditional practices, we no longer till up the vegetable garden each spring or fall. Instead, we practice lasagne layering, adding amendments appropriately and covering them with a final layer of compost. No-till farming is increasing in popularity as studies teach us the benefits of disturbing the soil colonies as little as possible.

Our ideas about compost have changed as well. Just a few years ago, only a handful of soil scientists thought of compost as anything but a cheap way to recycle garden wastes. Today, compost is viewed as the most important tool we have for encouraging healthy plant growth, as well as for healing exhausted or damaged soils. A new compost biodiversity rating scale has been developed, as have sophisticated methods for evaluating the quality and maturity of compost.

Seattle leads the country in working to reduce the urban waste stream by removing and utilizing green waste. Cedar Grove recycles Seattle's green waste into organically certified compost that is tested regularly for a full battery of pesticide residues as well as heavy metals, *E. coli*, and other contaminants. As Seattle learns, it shares the skills needed to produce compost of consistent quality with other communities. In time, urban composting and the regular use of compost will be common practices, making high-quality compost available in most if not all communities.

In my opinion, organic growing practices make good ecological sense. Organic food is good for our health, not only in terms of reducing adverse environmental impacts, but more directly. In several recent studies, organic foods tested out as nutritionally superior to conventionally grown food, the quality of which has declined by more than 20 percent over the past forty years (according to U.S. Department of Agriculture studies).

Organically grown food also tastes better, partly because organic farmers tend to choose specific types of vegetables and fruits for their flavor rather than their shipping quality. In addition, the use of compost promotes improved flavor as well as fragrance and color, since compost helps plants take in and store nutrients more efficiently. All these factors make organically grown foods taste better than most store-bought produce, especially the stuff trucked in from other states (or even other countries). When you consider that the average item on the grocery store shelf has traveled 1,100 miles to reach you, it becomes obvious that buying locally is smart for several reasons. Food that comes from nearby farms reaches you faster, so it's fresher. Local food also costs less to ship, saving gas and other forms of energy, including manpower.

Make a change

For many of us, entering a new century seemed like a logical time to take a good look at the way we live our lives. We may be thinking deeply about changing the way we eat for a whole range of reasons, of which health probably ranks high. Like New Year's resolutions, "new century" resolutions are easy to make but hard to keep. Rather than trying to make all kinds of changes at once, however, it's a good idea to work gradually toward the improvements we desire.

My kids and I have made the decision to eat,

A bonanza of basil, beans, snowpeas, celery, spinach, potatoes, petunias, peppers, 'Redbor' kale, pole beans, and corn.

Organic 'Early Girl' tomatoes.

based. However, we all agree that it is extremely important to support the most ecologically responsible farmers and growers.

As they grow up and become men, my kids and their friends have become increasingly aware of environmental damage. These days, they also care as much about the quality of what they eat as I do. They prefer organic food, as I do, for the health of their bodies and the health of the good earth. Yes, eating well can be expensive. However, eating poorly is also expensive, both up front and over the long term, as it affects our health and the health of the ecosystem.

If going organic overnight seems too big a leap for your budget or your diet, why not make a commitment to explore some of the exciting organic foods that are now widely available? Check out the produce department of your local grocery store, looking for locally grown organic foods. Visit the nearest farmer's market; talk with regional organic growers, and taste their wares. Best of all, consider growing some of your own food organically in your own backyard. I am willing to bet that you will be favorably impressed by the flavor and texture of organically grown food. That just might be the best benefit of all.

grow, or buy organic produce whenever possible. Our limited budget and the unlimited appetites of two teenagers and their friends tend to make many of my food shopping choices financially

Backyard deck of Eugene, Oregon, gardener, Sarah Robertson.

winter | *december january february*

In the maritime Northwest, winter begins in December, when the days draw in and the nights grow long. Although the vegetable garden is long since mulched and tidied up, a few brave patches of root crops keep company with the hardy herbs that can be gathered in snippets all year long. This dim season is full of holidays that celebrate light, and in the garden, too, the pale winter light comes as a gift, turning the last red cabbages to shimmering rubies and illuminating the great leaves of 'Bright Lights' chard like glowing stained glass.

If December speeds by, January crawls. January can be colder and more fierce than December, unleashing wild weather with all the potent energy of a fresh new year. But January is also famous for sudden, delicious thaws that fill the air with the enticing scent of warm, receptive earth. After a tempestuous demonstration of blustering bad temper, the soft chinook winds begin to blow, bringing milder weather and the warm, penetrating rains of spring in their wake.

*Overleaf: Garlic (*Allium sativum*); organic red beets.*

Though drab and often raw, February is full of promise. By the middle of February, the days are rapidly lengthening, and the evenings are beginning to stretch. Buds are swelling, bulbs are sprouting, and the soil is open and ready to work. By midmonth, we can prune roses, cut back the ornamental grasses, and start sowing hardy annuals.

Plant a living mulch to attract pollinators

I always carpet my vegetable beds with a living mulch of simple annual flowers to attract the pollinators that help swell the crops. Incomplete pollination is a huge problem where native and European honeybees have been lost to disease and pesticide exposure (zucchini that never finishes developing is a common example). To lure in the surviving bees, we need to offer a banquet of bloom in every season.

In the Northwest, this isn't too hard, even in a harsh year. Among my favorite pollinator plants is sweet alyssum, an easygoing annual that blooms long and hard with little care and self-sows ardently. Beloved by bees and other pollinators, this low grower boasts wave after wave of tiny, honey-scented white flowers. After you've grown alyssum once, you'll never be without a few volunteers, and you can nearly always find a sprig or two in bloom on any day of the year.

Another choice annual is calendula or calendar flower, so named for its habit of blooming at least a bit in every month. Typically yellow and orange, these sunny creatures come in vivid and soft citrus shades from near white to near red. Calendula petals are fed to hens to make the yolks of their eggs deep yellow. Used as garnish, the flowers add a pretty, peppery zest to soups and salads. Sow both of these tough beauties in February, either in flats or right where you want them to bloom.

Enjoy a winter harvest

The slow, cold months are not without riches. Our generally mild winter climate supports a delicious array of cold-season crops, from enduring greens like 'Siberian Red' kale and 'Quatre Saisons' lettuce to Brussels sprouts and leeks that sweeten with each frost.

Those who have a garden but don't work it year round may want to try some season-extending techniques that make it easy to enjoy fresh produce from the backyard. You don't need to invest great sums or lots of energy to create a protected, snug spot for a row of greens, a few fennel bulbs, some leeks, and a handful of hardneck garlic to refresh your meals through the coldest months.

Greenhouses are a delightful if expensive treat. In Alaska, I visited a small (heated) greenhouse outfitted with a cozy armchair and a reading lamp. The gardener who built it told me that she spent part of every day in her greenhouse during the long, dark winter months. She felt it saved her sanity to be around actively living plants, smelling fresh, warm earth and the sweet green scent of growing things.

In less extreme climates, even an unheated greenhouse offers a good deal of warmth and shelter for plants and gardeners. With a southwest exposure a simple lean-to greenhouse can support a terrific assortment of winter lettuces and greens, as well as corn salad and onion greens, parsley and chicory, endive and salsify. A heated garden room or greenhouse can keep cherry tomatoes productive all winter, as well as cilantro, basil, lemongrass, and ginger root. Add a chair and small table to either one, and odds are good that you, too, will find yourself gravitating to the company

of growing plants whenever you can squeeze in the time.

If you lack room or the budget for such luxuries, a set of cloches, a cold frame, or a simple tunnel hoop structure can keep you well stocked with greens even during a period of deep cold. Cloches or bell jars are dome-shaped plant covers made of glass, resin, fiberglass, or plastic. Clear or translucent, they allow light to reach plants, but keep them warm and relatively dry. Barn cloches are long enough to cover several plants. One company makes folding umbrella cloches on long stakes that can be driven into the ground. My cats loved to sneak under the edge and curl up in these, which made them less useful but highly decorative.

Cold frames come in many sizes and shapes, but all are essentially glass- or plastic-topped boxes without bottoms. Set to face south or southwest, these miniature unheated greenhouses capture all the sun that's available and may provide several degrees of extra warmth even without a cover. To reduce mold and mildew problems and increase air circulation, some models have open sides or tops that open automatically when the temperature inside the box reaches a preset level.

Mesclun mix.

A very simple cold frame can be made using four bales of straw and an old window, propped up a bit with a stout stick.

Inside the cold frame, a deep (12- to 18-inch) bed of compost and garden soil provides a sheltered, snug place to grow winter carrots, baby greens, spring onions, and so forth. If you are home a lot, you can remove or prop open the top of the cold frame daily, replacing it at night. This ensures a good flow of air, reducing losses to rots and mildews.

Hoop tunnels are made with half-hoops of flexible plastic pipe (or willow or dogwood twigs), each end stuck in the ground, to make a line of hoops at least 2 feet tall at the center. These hoops are then covered with a length of clear plastic or white woven row cover cloth, which lets in a bit less light but allows more natural air exchange while still providing several degrees of frost protection. At night, you can fold the ends of the tunnel down to close it up like a tent.

If you don't want to use plastic, you can make an inverted V-shaped structure using pairs of old windows, leaning them in against central posts or hinging them at the top. Secure the outer sides of the windows with rebar stakes or straw bales to keep them from slipping or blowing over in high winds.

The woven material sold as floating row cover can also be used all by itself to cover sturdy crops like kale, chard, leeks, fennel, and broccoli from heavy frost or snow. It is deeply satisfying to brush away the snow, pull open the cloth, and harvest a crisp salad on a bitterly cold day.

Without any extra protection at all, and even if your garden space is a modest balcony with room for just a few containers, you can still enjoy at least a modicum of fresh-from-the-garden produce in the depths of winter. Hardy herbs like rosemary, sage, thyme, and bay all grow well in containers and can be harvested throughout the winter months. In mild spells, you can gather fresh sprouts from your fall-planted onions and garlic, as well as sprigs of parsley and the tender new leaves of French sorrel. Even in tiny amounts, all will contribute refreshing savor and zest to your winter meals.

winter recipes

entrées

Rosemary Chicken
Creamy Risotto with Shrimp and Mustard Greens
Hazelnut Roasted Chicken and Potatoes
Curried Pork Loin with Dried Figs
Grilled Salmon with Beet and Orange Salsa
Crusty Baked Salmon with Curly Blue Kale

soups & stews

Italian Garlic Soup
Curried Turkey Soup
Potato Stew with Winter Greens
Kabocha Squash Soup with Caramelized Onions
Chase-Away-the-Flu Stew

side dishes

Swiss Chard with Bacon and Mustard Sauce
Hot Sweet Potato Salad
Savory Acorn Squash
Parsnips with Lime, Ginger, and Garlic
Thai Turnip Sauté with Sweet Chili Sauce
Two-Potato Pancakes

salads

Satsuma Salad
Winter Salad with Hot Cranberry Dressing
Confetti Slaw
French Winter Beet Salad
Winter Salad Supreme
Salsa Dressing

baked goods & sweets

Hazelnut-Cranberry Bread Pudding
Rosemary Bread
Orange-Rosemary Muffins
Ginger-Hazelnut Meringues
Flaming Pears with Ginger Sauce

Baby bok choi ('Meiquing').

winter menus

december
Italian Garlic Soup

Grilled Salmon with Beet
and Orange Salsa

Hot Sweet Potato Salad

Hazelnut-Cranberry Bread Pudding

january
Rosemary Chicken

Swiss Chard with Bacon and
Mustard Sauce

Orange-Rosemary Muffins

Flaming Pears with Ginger Sauce

february
Curried Pork Loin with Dried Figs

Confetti Slaw

Savory Acorn Squash

Ginger-Hazelnut Meringues

entrées

Rosemary Chicken

Crisp and golden, this roast chicken is deliciously fragrant with rosemary sprigs and thin lemon slices tucked under the skin before roasting. Use as the basis for the seasonal menu on page 7 or, for another serving idea, toss together a variety of root vegetables—perhaps parsnips, yams, carrots, and onions—with a little walnut or olive oil and fresh thyme, and set them in a shallow pan to roast alongside the bird. All you need to round them into a splendid dinner is a tossed salad of baby greens enriched with fresh herbs and onion greens.

1 roasting chicken, 3 to 4 pounds
1 organic lemon, thinly sliced
½ cup rosemary sprigs, cut in 1-inch pieces
1 tablespoon fresh rosemary leaves
2 tablespoons virgin olive oil
¼ teaspoon kosher or sea salt
½ teaspoon cracked peppercorns
2 large potatoes, peeled and quartered
2 large sweet potatoes or yams, peeled and quartered
2 turnips, peeled and quartered
2 carrots, peeled and halved lengthwise

■ Preheat the oven to 350°F. Make small cuts in the chicken skin just above the legs and gently insert the handle of a wooden spoon to loosen the skin. Slip the lemon slices and rosemary sprigs under the chicken skin.

■ In a baking or roasting pan large enough to hold the chicken, combine the rosemary leaves, olive oil, salt, and pepper. Roll the vegetables in the oil mixture to coat. Rub the remaining oil over the chicken and arrange in the pan with the vegetables. Roast until golden brown, about 1 hour.

MAKES 4 SERVINGS

Creamy Risotto with Shrimp and Mustard Greens

This saucy entrée is succulent with juicy shrimp. Shredded mustard greens, Chinese cabbage, and green peppercorns enliven the creamy rice.

2 tablespoons virgin olive oil
2 tablespoons butter
1 onion, finely chopped
2 cloves garlic, chopped
1 to 1½ cups Arborio rice
½ teaspoon salt
5 to 6 cups chicken or vegetable broth
1 pound cooked, peeled shrimp
2 teaspoons drained green peppercorns
1 bunch mustard greens, stemmed and shredded
1 small head bok choy or Chinese cabbage, shredded
1 cup cilantro or parsley leaves, for garnish

■ In a large saucepan, heat the olive oil and butter over medium heat until the butter melts. Add the onion and garlic and cook, stirring, until pale golden, 2 to 3 minutes. Add the rice and salt and cook, stirring, until rice is translucent, 2 to 3 minutes. Add 1 cup of the broth and cook, stirring, until the broth is absorbed. Add another ½ cup broth and repeat. Continue adding broth, ½ cup at a time, stirring constantly as each addition is absorbed.

■ After adding 5 cups, taste the rice; if it is still hard, continue adding broth and stirring until the rice is tender. The rice should be a bit soupy. Stir in the shrimp and green peppercorns, add the mustard greens and bok choy, cover the pan, and reduce the heat to low. Let sit over the heat for 2 to 3 minutes, then check the greens; when they are barely wilted, stir the greens into the risotto and serve, garnished with cilantro or parsley.

MAKES 4 TO 6 SERVINGS

Hazelnut Roasted Chicken and Potatoes

A golden crust of hazelnuts and herbs turns this fast, simple entrée into a gilded extravaganza fit for a party. The combination of sweet potatoes or yams with baking potatoes (any kind will do) gives this dish extra color as well as terrific flavor.

    6 fresh sage leaves
    1 teaspoon fresh rosemary leaves
    2 cloves garlic, chopped
    ½ cup toasted, skinned hazelnuts
    1 tablespoon virgin olive oil
    1 roasting chicken, 4 to 5 pounds
    4 large potatoes, peeled
    2 large sweet potatoes, peeled and cut in
      half
    ¼ teaspoon kosher or sea salt
    ¼ teaspoon freshly ground black pepper

■ Preheat the oven to 450°F. Chop the sage, rosemary, garlic, and hazelnuts into a rough paste and blend with the oil. Rub this mixture evenly over the chicken, potatoes, and sweet potatoes and place in a roasting pan. Sprinkle with the salt and pepper and place in the oven. Immediately reduce the heat to 350°F and roast until the chicken is tender and golden brown, about 1 hour.

Makes 4 servings

cook's tip

hazelnuts are rich in essential oils and lend their buttery flavor and tender crunch to both sweet and savory dishes. To rid them of their tight inner skins, spread them on a cookie sheet and toast them in a moderate (350°F) oven until lightly browned, about 20 minutes. Cool until you can handle them, then roll the nuts in a tea towel to loosen the papery skins. Toasted chopped nuts keep for up to a week in the refrigerator.

Curried Pork Loin with Dried Figs

Roll lean pork loin in garam masala, an Indian spice blend, and then slowly bake it to succulent, juicy perfection. When I was a kid, tender dried figs were available only during the winter holidays, often strung into "bracelets." Now they are easy to find in any season, yet they still taste best to me in hearty winter dishes.

1 lean pork loin roast, about 3 pounds
2 teaspoons virgin olive oil
2 to 3 teaspoons garam masala or curry powder
¼ cup chopped hazelnuts
3 cloves garlic, chopped
1 onion, chopped
2 stalks celery, chopped
12 dried figs
1 cup apple juice
1 lime, cut into wedges, for garnish

■ Preheat the oven to 350°F. Rub the pork lightly with ½ teaspoon of the olive oil, then roll it in the garam masala and hazelnuts. Heat the remaining 1½ teaspoons oil in a Dutch oven or an oven-safe pan over medium heat. Add the garlic, onion, celery, and figs and cook until soft, 3 to 5 minutes. Add the pork, turning it to brown quickly on all sides.

■ Add the apple juice, cover, and roast until the meat's juices run clear, 50 to 60 minutes or until internal temperature reaches 185°F. Let stand for 5 minutes, then slice thinly and serve, garnished with lime wedges.

MAKES 4 TO 6 SERVINGS

Grilled Salmon with Beet and Orange Salsa

This sizzling salmon is a knockout on the plate and on the palate. Lively with fresh lime and orange juices and smoky ancho chiles, the frisky beet salsa is an equally good match for chicken or pork.

1 teaspoon virgin olive oil
3 cloves garlic, chopped
¼ teaspoon salt
1 teaspoon fresh lemon thyme or any
   thyme leaves
1 teaspoon fresh rosemary leaves
½ teaspoon freshly ground black pepper
1½ pounds salmon fillet, skinned

Beet and Orange Salsa

½ red onion, chopped
2 cups cooked beets, diced (drained
   canned beets work fine)
1 red bell pepper, chopped
2 oranges, peeled and sectioned,
   membrane removed
¼ cup cilantro, stemmed
Juice and grated zest of 1 organic orange
Juice of 1 lime
2 to 4 tablespoons chopped ancho chiles
   (if using canned chiles, drain before
   measuring)
¼ teaspoon salt

■ Start coals in a grill or preheat the broiler. In a bowl, combine the olive oil, garlic, salt, lemon thyme, rosemary, and pepper. Rinse the salmon, pat it dry, and rub with the herbed oil mixture. Set aside.

■ To prepare the Beet and Orange Salsa, in a medium bowl gently toss the red onion, beets, bell pepper, orange sections, and cilantro with the orange juice and zest, lime juice, ancho chiles, and salt; set aside.

■ Grill or broil the salmon until opaque, 10 to 12 minutes. Cover tightly with foil and let sit for 10 minutes. Serve with the salsa.

Makes 4 servings

Winter greens, beets, and herbs.

Crusty Baked Salmon with 'Curly Blue' Kale

Zippy with fresh lime, this delicious baked salmon has a peppery rosemary crust and sits on a bed of crunchy 'Curly Blue' kale. You can, of course, use any kind of kale, depending on what looks best in the garden or at the market.

1½ pounds salmon fillet
1 teaspoon olive oil
1 teaspoon fresh rosemary leaves
1 teaspoon dried lavender flowers
½ teaspoon kosher salt
1 teaspoon cracked black peppercorns
½ cup bread crumbs
1 bunch 'Curly Blue' kale, trimmed and
   shredded, about 4 cups
1 red onion, finely chopped
1 lime, quartered, for garnish

■ Preheat the oven to 350°F. Rinse the salmon and pat it dry, then rub the skinless side with the olive oil. Set the fish, skinless side up, in a baking dish. In a small bowl, combine the rosemary, lavender, salt, peppercorns, and bread crumbs and pat over the fish. Bake until opaque, 25 to 30 minutes.

■ Arrange a bed of kale on each of 4 plates and top with the onion. Put a piece of the hot fish on each kale bed and serve, garnished with a lime wedge.

MAKES 4 SERVINGS

Curly kale amid flax.

soups
and stews

Italian Garlic Soup

If your family loves French onion soup, they'll appreciate this Italian soup redolent of garlic. Light but sumptuous, it can be made in less than half an hour. The vegetable broth made by Pacific Organic lends this soup an especially full body and rich finish.

8 cups vegetable broth

2 whole heads garlic, separated, peeled and lightly crushed

1 dried Italian peperoncino or any hot chile (either dried or fresh works fine)

1 bunch spinach, stemmed and shredded

1 bunch flat Italian parsley, stemmed

2 tablespoons virgin olive oil

8 thick slices Rosemary Bread (page 35) or other herb bread

1 cup grated Asiago or Romano cheese

■ Preheat the broiler. In a soup pot, bring the broth, garlic, and chile to a boil over high heat. Reduce the heat to medium and simmer for 10 minutes, then add the spinach and parsley.

■ Spoon out 8 of the garlic cloves and mash with the olive oil in a small bowl. Spread over one side of the bread slices and toast under the broiler. Ladle the soup into bowls, top each with three or four pieces of broken toast, and sprinkle with the grated cheese.

MAKES 4 TO 6 SERVINGS

Curried Turkey Soup

After a turkey fest, combine your holiday leftovers with fresh vegetables, broth, and mild tikka curry powder to make this enticing soup. Spicy yet subtle, it tastes even better if it sits overnight in the fridge.

1 tablespoon virgin olive oil

2 cloves garlic, chopped

½ onion, chopped

1 to 2 teaspoons tikka or sweet curry powder

4 stalks celery, chopped (with greens)

6 leaves kale, stemmed and shredded

2 cups coarsely chopped cooked turkey

1 cup cooked rice, stuffing, or mashed potatoes

4 cups vegetable broth

■ In a large saucepan, heat the olive oil, garlic, and onion over medium heat and cook, stirring, until barely soft, 2 to 3 minutes. Add the curry powder, celery, and kale, cover the pan, and cook to release the juices, 2 to 3 minutes. Add the turkey, rice, and broth. Reduce the heat to low, cover the pan, and heat through. Serve hot.

Makes 4 servings

Hardy Swiss chard.

Potato Stew with Winter Greens

I often serve this zesty, chile-laced stew around the winter solstice, when dark, leafy greens start tasting especially good. Like leeks, kale and chard get better when nipped by a light frost.

2 pounds organic 'Yellow Finn' potatoes, unpeeled, cut into quarters

3 cloves garlic, chopped

½ teaspoon fresh rosemary leaves

¾ teaspoon salt

¼ cup olive oil

1 or 2 jalapeño chiles, seeded and chopped

1 white or yellow onion, chopped

2 stalks celery, finely chopped

½ teaspoon ground cumin

¼ teaspoon ground cinnamon

3 cups stemmed, shredded kale

3 cups stemmed, shredded Swiss chard

1 bunch flat Italian parsley, stemmed, for garnish

■ Combine the potatoes, garlic, rosemary, and ½ teaspoon of the salt in a large saucepan. Add water to cover, then bring to a boil over medium-high heat. Reduce the heat to medium-low and simmer until tender, 15 to 20 minutes. Skim off any foam, and keep at a simmer over low heat.

■ In a soup pot, heat the olive oil over medium-high heat. Add the chiles, onion, and celery and cook, stirring, until barely soft, 4 to 5 minutes. Add the cumin, cinnamon, and salt to taste (start with ¼ teaspoon). Add the kale and chard, cover the pot, and cook until barely wilted, 3 to 4 minutes. Stir in the vegetables and broth and serve at once, garnished with the parsley.

MAKES 4 TO 6 SERVINGS

Kabocha Squash Soup with Caramelized Onions

Sweet and spicy flavors combine in a hearty soup that reminds some folks of Thai food. The sweetness of slow-cooked onions and squash is offset by an intriguing, currylike blend of coriander, nutmeg, ginger, and garlic.

- 1 small kabocha squash, 2 to 3 pounds, cut in half and seeded
- 1 tablespoon virgin olive oil
- 2 onions (about 2½ pounds), halved and sliced
- 2 cloves garlic, chopped
- 2-inch piece ginger root, peeled and chopped
- ½ teaspoon salt
- ¼ teaspoon sugar
- ¼ teaspoon ground coriander
- ¼ teaspoon ground nutmeg
- ¼ teaspoon *nanami togarashi* (Japanese chili powder) or any chili powder (optional)
- 4 cups vegetable broth, milk, or half-and-half
- ½ cup chopped green onions

■ Preheat the oven to 350°F. Place the squash, cut side down, in a baking pan, pour in an inch of water, and bake until fork-tender, 35 to 40 minutes. In a soup pot, heat the oil over medium-high heat and add the onions, garlic, ginger, salt, and sugar. Stir to coat the onions, and reduce the heat to low. Caramelize the onions slowly, stirring occasionally, until they turn deep golden brown, 30 to 40 minutes.

■ When the squash is tender, trim away the skin and cut the flesh into chunks. Add to the onions and mash lightly. Add the coriander, nutmeg, *nanami togarashi*, and broth and warm over medium-low heat. The soup will be chunky—if you prefer a smoother texture, purée it in batches in a blender or food processor to the desired consistency. Serve hot, topped with green onions.

MAKES 6 TO 8 SERVINGS

Gourds and winter squash on full display.

Chase-Away-the-Flu Stew

Winter brings all sorts of flu and colds to town. It seems that every culture has devised tasty stews and brews that seem to help keep illness at bay. Many share some common ingredients, from garlic to lemon and ginger. This garlic-rich version of chicken soup combines three kinds of onions (leeks, red onion, and green onion) with fresh ginger and garden herbs.

2 skinless boneless chicken breast halves

1 head garlic (about 10 cloves), separated and peeled

1 teaspoon fresh rosemary leaves

1 teaspoon salt

2 teaspoons virgin olive oil

2 leeks, thinly sliced (white and pale green parts only)

1 red onion, chopped

2-inch piece ginger root, peeled and chopped into medium pieces

2 stalks celery, chopped

1 teaspoon fresh lemon thyme leaves

10 leaves fresh sage, shredded

¼ cup flat Italian parsley leaves

Juice and grated zest of 1 organic lemon

2 cups chicken broth

8 to 10 ounces fresh noodles

1 bunch green onions, thinly sliced, for garnish

■ In a large saucepan, combine the chicken, 3 cloves of the garlic, ½ teaspoon of the rosemary, and ½ teaspoon of the salt. Add water to cover, bring to a boil over medium-high heat, reduce heat to medium, and simmer, covered, until chicken is tender, about 20 minutes. Remove from the heat, skim off the foam, and let cool.

■ In a soup pot, combine the olive oil, remaining garlic, leeks, red onion, ginger root, and celery and cook, stirring often, over medium-high heat until soft, 3 to 5 minutes. Add the thyme, sage, parsley, remaining ½ teaspoon rosemary, lemon juice and zest, and remaining ½ teaspoon salt and simmer over medium heat. Shred the chicken and add it to the pot, along with the chicken broth. Bring to a boil over medium-high heat, add the noodles, and cook, stirring, until tender, 3 to 5 minutes. Serve at once, garnished with the green onions.

Makes 2 to 4 servings

side dishes

Swiss Chard with Bacon and Mustard Sauce

Red stemmed and ruffled, Swiss chard is transformed by this succulent and savory bacon and mustard sauce. The same treatment is equally successful with spinach or kale, as well as with fennel and mushrooms.

    4 slices lean peppered bacon, chopped into 1-inch pieces
    1 small onion, chopped into medium dice
    1 teaspoon fresh marjoram or thyme leaves
    2 fresh sage leaves, shredded
    1 tablespoon red wine vinegar or cider vinegar
    1 tablespoon stone-ground, Dijon, or any sharp mustard
    8 cups shredded Swiss chard

■ In a large saucepan, cook the bacon over medium-high heat until golden but still soft. Remove to drain on a paper towel. Add the onion, marjoram, and sage to the pan and cook, stirring often, over medium heat until onion is pale golden, about 10 minutes. Add the vinegar and stir to deglaze the pan, loosening any stuck bits. Add the mustard and stir until smooth.

■ Bring the sauce to a gentle boil over medium-high heat, add the chard without stirring, and cover tightly. Reduce heat to medium and cook, covered, until chard is limp, 3 to 4 minutes. Stir the chard into the sauce and serve at once, garnished with the bacon.

MAKES 4 SERVINGS

cook's tip

Chard is packed with fiber, vitamins, and minerals, and is low in calories. To tame the earthy, slightly wild taste of chard, sizzle onions, garlic, or shallots in a teaspoon of olive oil, then add freshly washed, stemmed, and shredded chard. Cover the pan, let steam until the chard is wilted, and serve with a splash of fresh lime juice and a grind of pepper. A touch of fresh ginger root also enlivens plain winter chard, as will a handful of dried cranberries.

yams and sweet potatoes

It is challenging to grow yams and sweet potatoes in much of the Northwest, where cool nights keep soil temperatures low. Gardeners in Oregon's rich Willamette Valley may have better luck than their Northern counterparts, who will succeed best with container-grown plants (whisky barrels work quite well). Both tubers are very frost sensitive and can't be planted out until the soil feels like bath water (usually early summer). When buying yams and sweet potatoes at the market, look for fresh, young organic types that may be eaten raw, skin and all, in salads or diced into soups and stews.

For a scrumptious side dish, bake larger tubers whole with chicken or pork, splitting open the skins and drizzling the flesh with balsamic vinegar, fresh orange juice, or salsa. Peeled and chopped, both sweet potatoes and yams can be roasted with carrots, turnips, parsnips, and potatoes to accompany turkey or fish.

Hot Sweet Potato Salad

Next time you barbecue chicken or pork ribs, serve this potato salad on the side. Warm or chilled, the combination of 'Yukon Gold' potatoes with sweet potato chunks gives an old standby a charming Southern accent.

1½ pounds 'Yukon Gold' potatoes, peeled and cut into ½-inch dice
1½ pounds sweet potatoes, peeled and cut into ½-inch dice
1 teaspoon kosher or sea salt
2 to 3 teaspoons balsamic or red wine vinegar
½ cup mayonnaise (reduced-fat works fine)
½ cup sour cream (nonfat works fine)
2 tablespoons chopped flat Italian parsley
1 red onion, chopped
1 stalk celery, chopped
2 tablespoons chopped dill pickle (optional)
1 tablespoon drained capers (optional)
½ teaspoon coarsely ground black pepper

■ Combine the potatoes and sweet potatoes in a saucepan. Cover with water and add ¼ teaspoon of the salt. Bring to a boil over medium-high heat, reduce heat to medium-low, and simmer until fork-tender, 12 to 15 minutes. Skim off the foam, drain gently, and sprinkle the potatoes with the vinegar.

■ In a large bowl, combine the mayonnaise, sour cream, parsley, onion, and celery, along with the optional pickle and capers. Season to taste with the remaining ¾ teaspoon salt and the pepper. Add the potatoes and stir gently to coat. Serve warm, at room temperature, or chilled.

MAKES 4 TO 6 SERVINGS

Savory Acorn Squash

Serve this baked squash with roast turkey or pork, or let it be an unusual and tasty vegetarian entrée, complemented with steamed chard or spinach and a crisp salad spritzed with fresh lemon or lime juice.

2 acorn or Danish squash, trimmed, cut in
  half, and seeded
¼ cup orange juice concentrate
1 clove garlic, minced or pressed
2 tablespoons softened butter or olive oil
1 teaspoon kosher salt
1 teaspoon freshly ground black pepper

■ Preheat the oven to 350°F. Set the squash cut side down in a baking dish, and pour in 1 inch of water. Bake until squash is tender, 25 to 40 minutes. In a small bowl, combine the orange juice concentrate, garlic, butter, salt, and pepper.

■ Turn the squash cut side up and spoon some of the filling into each depression. Return to the oven and bake until the filling is bubbly. Serve hot.

MAKES 4 SERVINGS

Parsnips with Lime, Ginger, and Garlic

Why do people dread parsnips? Perhaps because when grown in poor soil, they taste like old sweat socks. Grow them yourself with plenty of compost, or buy organic parsnips, and prepare to be amazed. If you want to serve a greater variety of nutritious root crops, try this scintillating recipe, and when they ask you, "Wow! What is this?" just say it's a heritage European vegetable. This recipe is also terrific with carrots, yams, turnips, or kohlrabi.

3 parsnips, trimmed and peeled
½ to 1 teaspoon salt
1 tablespoon olive oil
3 or 4 cloves garlic, sliced
1-inch piece ginger root, peeled and sliced
Juice of ½ organic lime (cut the other half into wedges, for garnish)
1 to 3 tablespoons lime marmalade

■ Put the parsnips in a medium saucepan, add water to cover and ½ teaspoon salt, and bring to a boil over medium-high heat. Reduce the heat to medium and cook, uncovered, for 15 minutes. Drain, cut the parsnips in half, and slice, discarding the cores if woody.

■ Heat the olive oil in a frying pan over medium-high heat. Mince together the garlic and ginger root and add to the hot oil, stirring well. Cook for 1 minute, add the parsnips, and stir to coat. Add the lime juice and 1 tablespoon of the marmalade, then cook over medium-low heat for 10 minutes, stirring occasionally. Adjust the seasoning, adding more marmalade and salt to taste. Serve warm, garnished with lime wedges.

MAKES 4 SERVINGS

Thai Turnip Sauté with Sweet Chili Sauce

Thick, sweet-hot Thai chili sauce is usually used as a marinade for fish or fowl, though it's also great on turnips or any root crop, as well as any kind of meat. Brush it over thick slices of grilled eggplant for a delicious new treat.

1 tablespoon vegetable oil
3 cloves garlic, sliced
½ teaspoon salt
2 turnips, peeled and diced
1 to 3 tablespoons Thai sweet chili sauce

■ Heat the oil in a large frying pan over medium-high heat. Add the garlic and cook, stirring, for 1 minute, then add the salt and turnips, stirring to coat. Cook until turnips are tender, 4 to 5 minutes, then add sweet chili sauce to taste (start with 1 tablespoon). Serve hot.

MAKES 4 SERVINGS

winter-harvest vegetables

mild winters are wonderful for ornamental gardeners, but they're a bit frustrating for those who savor the sweetness that a touch of frost lends to winter-harvested vegetables like parsnips, Brussels sprouts, and leeks. Many people have an aversion to winter root crops, but I've found that even parsnip haters will happily eat Parsnips with Lime, Ginger, and Garlic (page 24), as long as I don't tell them what they are eating.

The sweet-hot principle works wonders with winter root crops that combine sweet and peppery flavors themselves. Parsnips, turnips, and Brussels sprouts are all tasty when served with a quick sauce of garlic sautéed in oil with a dab of apricot pepper jam. For a new twist, try serving frost-nipped parsnips with a sizzling Thai sweet-hot curry sauce. Not convinced? Try just one small batch and see if you don't become a convert.

Two-Potato Pancakes

Delightfully rich and savory, these pancakes cook up crisp and golden in a mixture of olive oil and butter, but you can skip the butter if you like. For a change, try blending in parsley or sage instead of thyme, and garnish with garlic-spiked yogurt and cilantro for a bit more zip.

2 medium potatoes, peeled and coarsely grated

1 medium yam, peeled and coarsely grated

1 tablespoon whole wheat pastry flour or any flour

½ teaspoon fresh lemon thyme or any thyme leaves

2 cloves garlic, chopped

¼ onion, finely chopped

¼ teaspoon kosher or sea salt

¼ teaspoon freshly ground black pepper

1 tablespoon virgin olive oil

1 tablespoon butter

½ cup sour cream (nonfat works fine), for garnish

¼ cup flat Italian parsley leaves, chopped, for garnish

New crop potatoes.

■ Gently stir together the grated potatoes, grated yam, flour, thyme, garlic, onion, salt, and pepper.

■ In a frying pan, heat the olive oil and butter over medium-high heat. Add the potato mixture by the heaping tablespoon and cook until brown on both sides, 3 to 4 minutes per side, turning once. Serve warm, garnished with sour cream and parsley.

MAKES 4 SERVINGS

salads

Satsuma Salad

Sparkling with flavor, this refreshing satsuma salad rounds out any meal. Marinate the satsuma sections in rice vinegar, then tumble them with chunks of apple and toasted peanuts over crunchy bok choy and velvety young spinach.

¼ cup rice vinegar
1 tablespoon peanut oil or vegetable oil
½ teaspoon shoyu or citrus soy sauce
1 clove garlic, minced or pressed
1 to 2 tablespoons fresh orange juice
1 cup satsuma sections (about 4 satsumas)
1 stalk celery, thinly sliced
1 tart apple, unpeeled, cored and chopped
1 or 2 heads baby bok choy, thinly sliced
   (about 2 cups)
1 bunch young spinach, stemmed
2 tablespoons peanuts or sesame seeds,
   toasted

■ In a medium bowl, combine the vinegar, oil, shoyu, garlic, and orange juice to taste. Add the satsuma sections, celery, and apple; set aside for at least half an hour (or overnight in the fridge).

■ When ready to serve, heap the bok choy and spinach in a salad bowl. Add the satsuma dressing and toss lightly. Top with peanuts or sesame seeds and serve at once.

Makes 4 servings

Organic winter salad greens.

Winter Salad with Hot Cranberry Dressing

This delightful salad sings to your senses, providing a deliciously different accompaniment for anything from roast pork to grilled fish. The sparkling dressing is also terrific over steamed vegetables or roast chicken.

2 cups (about 8 leaves) thinly sliced savoy cabbage
2 cups shredded spinach leaves
4 satsuma oranges, peeled and sectioned
½ cup cashews, toasted
1 Walla Walla Sweet or red Bermuda onion, chopped

Hot Cranberry Dressing

4 strips bacon, chopped, or 1 tablespoon olive oil
3 cloves garlic, chopped
2 cups cranberries, rinsed and picked over
½ cup water
About 6 ounces orange juice concentrate
About ¼ teaspoon kosher or sea salt
About ¼ teaspoon freshly ground black pepper

■ Toss the cabbage and spinach together in a large salad bowl. Scatter the satsumas, cashews, and half the onion over the leaves.

■ To prepare the Hot Cranberry Dressing, in a frying pan, cook the bacon over medium-high heat until crisp and brown. Remove the bacon from the pan and drain on a paper towel. Pour off all but 1 tablespoon of the bacon drippings, add the garlic, and cook, stirring, until pale golden, 3 to 5 minutes. Add the cranberries and water, bring to a boil, reduce the heat, cover, and simmer until the cranberries pop, about 7 to 8 minutes.

■ Remove the cover, increase the heat to medium-high, and cook, stirring often, until the liquid is reduced by half. Stir in the orange juice concentrate, 1 tablespoon at a time, until the sweet-tart balance tastes just right. Season to taste, starting with ⅛ teaspoon each of salt and pepper. Toss the dressing with the salad and serve immediately.

MAKES 4 TO 6 SERVINGS

how to buy oranges

the brief satsuma season is cause for celebration in the Northwest, where they generally arrive in time to enliven winter holiday meals. Large satsumas are nearly always sweeter than the smaller ones, which can be quite sour, especially early in the shipping season.

Those blessed with sunny houses or greenhouses can grow citrus well in the Northwest, but most of us must buy oranges at the market. It's an excellent idea to buy only organic fruit whenever you plan to use the rind of any citrus, to avoid ingesting pesticide residues that are not intended for human consumption. Don't worry if organic citrus fruits have a few blemishes; they won't affect the flavor at all and the zest tastes fine no matter what it looks like.

When choosing oranges or any citrus fruit, cup several in your hand one by one. The heaviest fruit will be the juiciest and most flavorful. Ripe fruit often has a slight fragrance, while underripe fruit has little or no fruity scent.

Confetti Slaw

Fresh, vivid colors and clear contrasts of flavor make this shredded salad as pretty in the bowl as it is lively on the palate. You can substitute an assortment of cabbages in this recipe, including sweet-hot bok choy and wrinkled savoy cabbage.

1 cup shredded red cabbage
1 cup shredded green cabbage
½ cup yogurt (nonfat is fine)
½ cup mayonnaise (reduced-fat is fine)
1 to 2 teaspoons balsamic vinegar
1 clove garlic, peeled and pressed or minced
¼ to ½ teaspoon salt
¼ to ½ teaspoon freshly ground black pepper
1 firm red dessert apple (Braeburn or Cox's), grated
1 small red onion, finely chopped
¼ cup peeled, coarsely grated young sweet carrots
¼ cup flat Italian parsley or cilantro leaves, for garnish

■ Soak the red and green cabbage in very cold water for half an hour or more. In a mixing bowl, blend the yogurt, mayonnaise, 1 teaspoon vinegar, garlic, ¼ teaspoon salt, and ¼ teaspoon pepper. Let sit for 15 minutes, then adjust the vinegar, salt, and pepper to taste.

■ When the cabbage is crisp, drain well and toss with the dressing, along with the apple, onion, and carrot, in a large bowl. Serve at once, garnished with parsley.

MAKES 4 SERVINGS

Winter Salad Supreme

This refreshing mixture of young greens, shredded bok choy, and sweet satsumas is very lovely, but the sumptuous basil-avocado dressing makes it fabulous. Try the dressing on an ordinary salmon sandwich or in chicken salad for an unforgettable meal.

4 satsuma oranges, peeled and sectioned
¼ cup rice vinegar
½ cup olive oil
1¼ cups shredded fresh basil leaves
1 to 2 cloves garlic, chopped
¼ teaspoon kosher salt
1 tablespoon balsamic vinegar
¼ teaspoon freshly ground black pepper
4 cups mixed baby greens
1 cup shredded bok choy
¼ cup cilantro leaves
¼ cup flat Italian parsley leaves
1 ripe avocado, cut into chunks

■ In a medium bowl, marinate the satsuma sections in the rice vinegar for at least half an hour in the refrigerator (overnight or all day is fine). At serving time, combine the olive oil, 1 cup of the basil, garlic, salt, balsamic vinegar, and pepper in a food processor or blender and process into a thick paste.

■ In a salad bowl, combine the baby greens, bok choy, cilantro, parsley, and the remaining ¼ cup basil. Toss the satsuma sections and avocado chunks with the basil-oil mixture, pour over the salad greens, toss gently, and serve.

MAKES 4 SERVINGS

French Winter Beet Salad

This was inspired by a salad I was served on a barge trip up the Loire Valley. Terrific with grilled salmon or roast pork, this beet salad combines good looks with vivid flavors. If you are out of garden beets, use canned ones, well drained. Any crisp apple will do in this recipe, though both Braeburn and Granny Smith are excellent choices.

> 3 crisp eating apples, peeled, cored, and diced
> Juice of 1 organic lemon
> 1½ cups diced cooked beets
> 1 cup walnut halves, toasted
> 1 bunch flat Italian parsley, stemmed, for garnish

Dressing

> Grated zest of 1 organic lemon
> 2 tablespoons walnut or wine vinegar
> ½ cup walnut oil or virgin olive oil
> 1 tablespoon Dijon or homemade mustard
> ¼ teaspoon kosher or sea salt
> ¼ teaspoon freshly ground black pepper

- To prepare the dressing, in a jar, combine lemon zest, vinegar, oil, mustard, salt, and pepper. Cover tightly, shake well to emulsify, and set aside.

- In a serving bowl, toss the apples gently with the lemon juice. Add the beets and walnuts, toss again with the dressing, and serve garnished with parsley.

MAKES 4 TO 6 SERVINGS

Salsa Dressing

Any greens taste great when drizzled with this snappy dressing, which also dresses up grilled or baked salmon nicely. Emerald Valley makes a delightful fresh salsa that works very well in this recipe, or substitute your own favorite.

> ½ cup rice vinegar
> Juice and grated zest of 1 organic orange
> ½ cup medium salsa

- In a jar, combine the vinegar, orange juice, orange zest, and salsa. Shake well and serve. Refrigerate any leftover dressing.

MAKES ABOUT I CUP

baked goods and sweets

Hazelnut-Cranberry Bread Pudding

When the winter blues attack, fend them off with a bowl of this bread pudding, coupled with a hot bath and a good book. If you have small individual casserole dishes, you can make single servings, or bake a bigger batch to share.

> 1 cup milk (nonfat works fine), or 1 cup vanilla soymilk
> 1 to 2 tablespoons honey
> Few grains nutmeg
> 1 cup cubed multigrain bread (small cubes)
> 1 egg, slightly beaten
> 1 tablespoon dried cranberries
> 1 tablespoon hazelnuts, toasted, skinned, and chopped
> 1 tablespoon brown sugar

■ Preheat the oven to 350°F. In a small pan, bring the milk to a simmer over medium heat. Add the honey and stir until dissolved, then add the nutmeg. Place the bread cubes in a medium bowl and pour the milk mixture over them. Let sit for 10 minutes.

■ Stir in the egg and cranberries. Divide between 2 individual casseroles or place in a 1-quart baking dish. Top with the nuts and brown sugar and bake until set and lightly browned, 35 to 40 minutes.

MAKES 2 SERVINGS

cook's tip

1ocally grown cranberries can be purchased from mid-November through January. Organic cranberries are becoming a specialty in Oregon and parts of Washington, and frozen organic cranberries can be found year-round in supermarkets. When used in baking, dried cranberries infused with sugar or honey may be preferred over fresh berries by those who don't care for very tart fruit. Experiment with cranberries by substituting them in recipes that call for rhubarb, from chutney or pie to sorbet or cobbler.

Rosemary Bread

Rosemary is traditionally used with roast fowl or pork, but it also tastes great in bread or rolls. Serve this bread warm with soup or stew, slice it thinly for smoked salmon sandwiches, or cut thick slices for crunchy toast points to set under the year's first asparagus.

> 1 cup hot water
> 1 envelope (1 scant tablespoon) dry yeast
> 1 teaspoon sugar
> 1 teaspoon salt
> 1 tablespoon chopped fresh rosemary leaves
> 2 tablespoons olive oil, divided
> 1 cup whole wheat pastry flour
> 1 to 1½ cups unbleached white flour
> 1 tablespoon cornmeal
> 1 teaspoon kosher or sea salt

■ In a mixing bowl, combine the hot water with the yeast and sugar. Let sit for 5 minutes, until yeast is soft, then add the salt, rosemary, 1 tablespoon of the olive oil, and the whole wheat flour. Stir into a soft paste, then add 1 cup of the unbleached flour to make a soft dough. Rub the dough ball with 1 teaspoon olive oil. Cover the bowl with a cloth and let rise until doubled in bulk, about 30 minutes.

■ Punch down the dough, add 1 teaspoon olive oil, and knead (pushing it with a rolling motion), adding flour as needed if the dough feels sticky. Knead until the dough blisters and then becomes smooth and feels elastic, about 5 minutes.

■ Preheat the oven to 425°F. Sprinkle a baking sheet with the cornmeal. Rub the dough ball with the remaining 1 teaspoon olive oil and sprinkle with the kosher salt. Set on the baking sheet, slash the top of the dough 2 or 3 times with a sharp knife (penetrating about ½ inch), and let the dough rise again. When it has doubled in bulk, bake for 10 minutes.

■ Reduce the heat to 350°F and bake until the loaf is golden and sounds hollow when tapped, about 25 minutes. Cool for 10 minutes before slicing.

MAKES 1 ROUND LOAF

Orange-Rosemary Muffins

A basket of these muffins, warm from the oven, makes any meal special. If you prefer, use fresh sage or lemon thyme instead of rosemary and add some toasted walnuts for extra crunch.

1 cup whole wheat pastry flour
1 cup unbleached white flour
2 teaspoons baking powder
½ teaspoon salt
1 tablespoon sugar
2 eggs, beaten
¼ cup vegetable oil
Juice and grated zest of 1 organic orange
2 teaspoons chopped rosemary leaves
½ to ¾ cup milk

■ Preheat the oven to 400°F. Line 12 muffin cups with paper liners. Sift together the flours, baking powder, salt, and sugar into a bowl.

■ In a larger bowl, beat the eggs with the oil until well mixed, then stir in the orange juice and zest, rosemary, and ½ cup milk. Gently stir in the dry ingredients; do not overmix. Add up to ¼ cup more milk if the batter is too thick; it should be the consistency of heavy cream.

■ Spoon into the muffin cups, filling them one-half to three-fourths full. Bake until golden brown, 20 to 25 minutes. Serve warm.

MAKES 12 MUFFINS

Ginger-Hazelnut Meringues

Light, crunchy, and fat-free, these cookies provide a grand finale to any meal. When you're in a stay-at-home mood, mix them up in the morning and let them cook while you knit or read by the fire. I added candied ginger and toasted nuts, but you can use bits of crushed peppermint sticks, tiny chocolate chips, or crushed brittle if you prefer.

> 2 egg whites, at room temperature
> Pinch of salt
> ⅔ cup sugar, sifted
> ¼ teaspoon vanilla extract
> 2 tablespoons finely chopped crystallized ginger
> 2 tablespoons hazelnuts, toasted, skinned, and chopped

■ Preheat the oven to 250°F. Line 2 baking sheets with foil or baking parchment. In a deep bowl, combine the egg whites and salt and beat with an electric mixer until soft peaks form. Slowly add the sugar, a tablespoon at a time, beating constantly. When the egg whites are stiff but not dry, gently fold in the vanilla, crystallized ginger, and nuts.

■ Drop by teaspoonfuls onto the cookie sheets or use a pastry bag to pipe rosettes, using a ½-inch star tip. Bake until dry but not brown, 45 to 50 minutes. Cool to room temperature before removing from the pans. Store in a tightly sealed tin.

MAKES ABOUT 4 DOZEN MERINGUES

Flaming Pears with Ginger Sauce

I invented this impressively handsome dish for my son Andrew's January birthday. Each serving is garnished with its own little candle. (That's where the flame comes in.) Flame on!

3 red winter pears, halved and cored
2 cups apple cider or juice
2-inch piece ginger root, peeled and
   chopped
¼ cup chopped crystallized ginger
1 teaspoon vanilla extract
2 to 3 teaspoons sugar (optional)
3 cups vanilla ice cream

■ Preheat the oven to 350°F. Place the pears cut-side down in a baking pan large enough to hold them. In a saucepan, combine the apple cider, ginger root, crystallized ginger, vanilla, and sugar, if using. Bring to a boil and pour over pears. Cover the pan tightly with foil and bake until the pears are soft, about 30 minutes.

■ Lift the pears onto a serving platter and pour the sauce back into the saucepan. Reduce the sauce over medium-high heat, stirring, until about 1 cup remains. Taste and adjust the seasoning if needed (you may want a bit more sugar or vanilla). Put a scoop of ice cream in each pear half, top with sauce and a birthday candle, and serve, accompanied by extra sauce.

MAKES 3 TO 6 SERVINGS

No Cold Tea

Colds seem to vanish faster when I drink lots of this tea. It combines thyme, which has natural disinfectant properties, with rosemary, sage, and fresh ginger root. It's especially tasty made with lemon thyme.

   2 tablespoons fresh lemon thyme or any
      thyme leaves
   1 tablespoon fresh rosemary leaves
   1 tablespoon shredded fresh sage leaves
   1-inch piece ginger root, peeled and
      grated
   2 cups boiling water
   1 teaspoon honey, plus more to taste

■ In a saucepan, combine the thyme, rosemary, sage, ginger root, and boiling water. Cover and let steep for 20 minutes.

■ Strain, sweeten to taste with honey (start with 1 teaspoon), and serve.

MAKES 2 CUPS

winter gardening calendar

what to plant	Nothing, really.
what to harvest	Beets, broccoli, Brussels sprouts, cabbage, carrots, garlic, kale, leeks, onions, parsnips, potatoes, spinach, Swiss chard, turnips, winter lettuces, winter squash
what's in the market	Apples, cranberries, hazelnuts, pears, pomegranates, satsumas, winter greens, winter squash

gardening notes for winter ingredients

■ *Acorn and Other Winter Squash* Winter squash are tropical crops that prefer late-spring or early-summer planting in a warm, sunny spot with well-drained soil amended with copious amounts of compost. A deep (3- to 4-inch) compost mulch also helps retain soil moisture, which is critical to the proper filling out and ripening of winter squash. Use soaker hoses to avoid wetting the big leaves, which are very susceptible to mildews if wet.

Squash require a lot of room and deep soil or mounded beds to grow properly. Each sprawling plant can produce many smaller squash or a few really big ones; pick off tiny fruit to reduce the number and get larger ones if that's your preference.

Hard-shelled winter squash have an essential sweetness that works well in both sweet and savory recipes. The harder the skin, the longer winter

Mixed gourds and pumpkins.

squash will keep. In storage, check them periodically for soft spots. Most often, winter squash are cut in half and seeded and then baked or steamed. The softened pulp is then scooped out and diced or mashed for use in a wide variety of recipes, from soups and side dishes to pies and ice cream.

■ *Beets* Like all root crops, beets flourish in deep, fertile, well-drained soil. Gardeners with heavy soil will have the best results growing beets in mounded beds that are well amended with compost and grit or crushed sand. Beet seeds are really clusters, so each one sends up a little bouquet of sprouts. To avoid damaging the roots (undesirable in a root crop), remove the extra sprouts by snipping them off with nail scissors.

If you prefer beet greens, let the whole bunch grow and you can start harvesting the leaves as soon as they are the size of a soup spoon. Start by taking off the outer leaves first, and always remove less than you leave to encourage future growth.

A cool-weather crop, beets can be started in late summer for fall and early- to midwinter harvest or in late winter and early spring for early- to midsummer eating. Whether round or cylindrical, red, golden, white, or striped, all beets taste pretty similar. Here in the Northwest, small beets like 'Kestrel' often outperform the huskier versions that thrive where nights are warmer. Beautiful 'Golden' combine a wine-red skin with rich golden flesh, while the Italian favorite, 'Chioggia', with candy-cane red-and-white striped flesh, looks gorgeous sliced into salads.

The highly nutritious roots and greens can be eaten raw when young, and roasted, boiled, steamed, or stir-fried when mature. Boil whole beets unpeeled to keep from staining enameled cookware (the skins make a lovely golden dye, even those from red beets).

■ *Cabbage and Choys* Most years, Northwestern gardeners can harvest late cabbages from fall through late winter and early ones from midspring to early summer. Early cabbages are fast growers, needing only compost-rich soil and adequate moisture to form handsome heads within a couple of months. Late cabbages may take 3 to 4 months to head up fully and will continue growing (very slowly) despite lower temperatures. Try a mix of red and green cabbages, and avoid a glut by sowing seeds in flats and then setting out seedlings a few at a time, 3 to 4 weeks apart.

Asian choys are also cool-weather crops that

taste sweetest in fall and early winter. Bok choy and joi choy are also good performers in early spring, when the sweet-hot leaves can be shredded into salads, stir-fries, soups, and stews. Like cabbages, the choys must be harvested as whole plants. Remove the tough outer leaves and use the tender inner ones raw or lightly cooked.

Good cabbage choices for Northwestern gardeners include the glowing, lustrous 'Ruby Ball'; crisp, sweet 'Parel' (a Dutch type); and a long-lasting French variety called 'Charmant'.

■ *Garlic* Garlic grows beautifully in the Northwest, as long as it's given well-drained soil. Add lots of compost as well as grit or crushed sand to clay-based beds, and always plant garlic (and all its allium relatives, from chives to onions and shallots) in mounded beds that allow air to reach the roots. In the Northwest, garlic can be planted in fall for winter and spring harvest and in early spring for summer and fall harvest.

In the fall, you'll find a good variety of both softneck and hardneck garlic sets for sale, while in spring you'll find more softneck types. The typical grocery store garlic is a softneck type with papery white wrappings and a sharp flavor. Gourmet cooks often prefer the wider range of flavors, from mild to fiery, available in hardneck garlics like 'Nootka Rose', 'Spanish Roja', and 'Siberian'. Hardneck garlics tend to have rosy or pinkish brown wrappers and don't store as well as the softnecks.

The shoots of fall-planted garlic can be gathered in moderation all winter long. These rounded, tubular stems are like a cross between giant chives and green onions, with a decidedly garlic-laden flavor. Snipped into tiny bits, garlic greens can be used in soups and salads and to garnish entrées and side dishes. (See also Elephant Garlic, page 93.)

■ *Hazelnuts* Although our native hazelnuts are edible and quite tasty, Oregon's commercial crops are generally European hazelnuts, also called filberts. It is best to plant two kinds of filberts for optimal pollination, though you may not need to if native hazelnuts abound in your area. These handsome large shrubs or small trees appreciate a sunny spot in well-drained soil, and do best in mounded beds in heavier soils. If you plant your own filberts, give them plenty of room; unlike our native shrubs, European filberts may reach 20 feet in height and canopy spread. Expect to wait a few years for a substantial crop; you may get only

'Derby Day' cabbage.

a pound or two until your trees are 6 to 8 years old, and then you may get 20 pounds of nuts. Be aware that the ornamental contorted filbert called 'Harry Lauder's Walking Stick' is infected with a virus that causes its contortion. This virus is highly contagious and can cause nut crops to fail, so don't plant your productive trees within ¼ mile of a contorted one.

■ *Kale* Durable and easy to grow in well-drained soil amended with compost, kale is one of the best crops for Northwestern gardeners. To harvest twice a year, sow seed in May and again in early July, keeping rows about 18 inches apart and thinning plants (eat the babies in salads) to about 24 inches apart. Harvest the outer leaves when they are hand-sized or larger, but leave the inner core to keep the plant growing strongly.

Beautiful as well as delicious, kale comes in lovely colors and textures that earn their place in ornamental borders as well as vegetable beds. Curly Scotch kales are best eaten young, while the Russian and Siberian types remain tender through the winter. Among the best are 'Curly Blue', 'Black Dragon', 'White Russian', 'Redbor', 'Siberian Red', and 'Nero di Toscana' (also called 'Tuscan Black').

Grow leeks in two crops to enjoy year-round.

■ *Leeks* Sturdy and disease resistant, leeks are sometimes used to repel pests like aphids in rose gardens (the flowers are really quite beautiful). Leeks prefer well-drained soil amended and mulched with plenty of compost and do best with early, light feeding. To enjoy leeks through the year, grow two crops, sowing seeds indoors in late winter and transplanting in late April or early May. Space rows about 18 inches apart and thin plants to 6 to 8 inches apart. Plant starts in April and May and again in July for fall and winter harvest.

For many years, I've grown a savory heritage leek called 'Italian Purple', which has a burnished burgundy stem and outer leaves. However, newer varieties like 'Tadorna' and 'Sheriff' are easier to find (and clean), so now I grow and enjoy them all. Why not?

■ *Mustard Greens* Fast-growing mustard greens come plain or fancy, with broad or frilled foliage in green or burgundy red. Seedlings set out in fall may be harvested through most winters and will grow happily through hard frosts with a little protection (perhaps a cold frame or a cloche). Seed sown in early spring can be harvested as soon as the young plants are about 6 inches tall;

pick the outer leaves first, and always remove less than you leave to encourage regrowth. To enjoy mustard greens all year, sow a short row every few weeks; in all but the hottest and coldest weather, the young plants will thrive.

Sometimes called mustard spinach, mustard greens can be steamed, stir-fried, or shredded into soups, salads, and stews. Serve steamed or grilled fish on a bed of finely cut mustard greens, or use shredded mustard greens as a lively garnish for chicken or pork.

The mustard family includes numerous succulent varieties of leafy greens that add snap to salads, soups, and stir-fries. Oriental mustard greens like shiso, 'Osaka Red', 'Mizuba', and 'Tah Tsai' have a gentle bite that enlivens plain lettuce with panache. 'Green Wave' and 'Giant Red' have zippier young leaves and mellow mature ones, and both make very handsome ornamental border plants.

■ *Parsnips* Very easy to grow, parsnips achieve the finest flavor when grown in well-drained soil amended and mulched with lots of compost. These old-fashioned root vegetables are related to carrots, producing a long, cone-shaped storage root that may be white or yellow. Sow parsnips in late winter (under cover), and early spring for fall and winter harvest, and in fall for spring and summer harvest. Soak the seeds for a few hours in cool water, then sow in rows where they will grow (root crops don't transplant cheerfully).

Parsnips taste best in late fall and winter, when sweetened by a touch of frost. Peel parsnips and chunk them into stews, grate them into soups, or roast them with other root vegetables as a side dish.

■ *Pears* Pear trees do well in the Northwest, tolerating heavy soils and cool nights better than many other fruit trees. In most cases, it's best to grow two or more varieties of pear to ensure cross-pollination and fruit set. To avoid frost damage to blossoms, place trees on high or sloping ground and in as much sun as possible.

Though a fall crop, most late-ripening pears are splendid keepers. Picked slightly green and very firm in September or October, late pears continue to ripen in storage, reaching a peak of perfection in early winter to midwinter. Ruddy-skinned 'Beurre d'Anjou' is an exceptionally good keeper, as are golden-russet 'Comice' and greeny-gold 'Winter Nelis'.

■ *Potatoes* Potatoes are among the easiest of crops, especially if you can offer them a sunny, well-composted bed that drains freely. Although commercial crops require lots of pesticides, it's easy to grow healthy crops at home without any toxic treatments. The trick is to give potatoes excellent drainage. Those with heavy clay soils can grow them best in mounded beds amended with grit or crushed sand and ample compost.

Spring is the best time to start potatoes. To plant, cut potato starts into 1- to 2-inch chunks, each of which should have at least two "eyes" or sprouting points. Let them dry for a day or two, then plant them about 2 inches deep, placing the pieces 1 to 2 feet apart (depending on the size of the potato variety). You may also use small seed potatoes that don't need to be cut. You can begin harvesting new potatoes within 90 days, though large potatoes may take a bit longer to mature.

Since they may harvest 20 to 25 pounds of potatoes for each pound of seed potatoes planted, most gardeners prefer to plant small amounts of several (or many) types. Choose from white-, red-, brown-, yellow-, or blue-skinned potatoes, with creamy, white, yellow, or blue insides. If you like potato salad, look for fingerling types

*Rosemary (*Rosmarinus officinalis *'Christmas').*

like 'Lady Finger' and 'Yellow Finn'. For richer flavor, try 'Yukon Gold' or 'Peruvian Blue'.

■ *Rosemary* This enduring Mediterranean herb is also an excellent ornamental evergreen. Give rosemary a sunny spot with good air circulation, and you are almost guaranteed success. Long-lived and drought tolerant, rosemary comes in a range of sizes and shapes, from prostrate creepers like 'Irene' to scramblers like 'Severn Seas', bushy uprights like 'Arp', and slim, columnar forms like 'Tuscan Blue'. There are dozens of rosemary selections in cultivation, with scents and flavors that vary from meltingly mild to harsh and resinous.

Rosemary grows best with benign neglect, preferring compost over fertilizer and thriving without supplemental summer water, once established. Of the uprights, those with the darkest blue flowers (like 'Arp') tend to be the hardiest. The low-growing rosemaries are the least hardy, and are apt to vanish after prolonged cold snaps or to rot out in excessively wet winters.

You can harvest rosemary all year round, taking both twig tips and larger branches as needed. Cutting your plant back lightly will promote bushiness, but shearing can make plants too dense, causing the inner branches to defoliate.

■ *Swiss Chard* Vigorous and tough, chard is a classic winter crop that grows readily through all but the coldest Northwestern winters. A relative of the beet, chard is easy to please in almost any kind of soil, appreciating generous additions of mature compost rather than fertilizer. Start plants from seed or buy seedlings in spring or fall, setting them 12 to 18 inches apart. You can start to harvest the older, outer leaves when the young plants are about a foot tall. To encourage regrowth, always leave more than you remove.

While many forms of Swiss chard are green with white veins and ribbing, rosy 'Rhubarb' chard offers large, lush leaves with ruby red stems, and the brilliant 'Bright Lights' strain brings a rainbow of colors to the garden. Sow a patch and you'll find seedlings with red, pink, yellow, orange, white, purple, or green stems and lovely, strongly veined leaves to match. A few growers now offer selected colors from the 'Bright Lights' series, which are highly prized by flower arrangers. All taste great, so mix and match as you please.

■ *Turnips* All root crops, including turnips, need well-drained soil amended with ample compost. Where clay is heavy, plant in raised or mounded beds at least 12 inches deep. Sow seed every few weeks from May through August for fall and winter harvest, keeping rows about 18 inches apart. Thin young plants to 6 inches apart (add younglings to salads). Where flea beetles and root maggots are an issue, cover the whole row with a floating row cover material such as Reemay, securing it with earth staples every 6 inches. Keep the material loose enough so that the plants can grow as tall as they need to (about 18 inches).

Like carrots, turnips may be kept in the ground and harvested through the winter. Harvest the sweet, young turnips whenever you like. If you can't beat the root pests, just gather the delectable turnip greens throughout the growing season and add them to stir-fries, salads, soups, and stews. In the Northwest, best bets include the classic 'Purple Top White Globe' and the newer 'Shogoin'.

Vegetable garden bursting with Brussels sprouts, snapdragons, and white Kohlrabi.

spring | *march april may*

After the dreary, dripping days of February, March blows in with bluster and a blessing, sweeping away the tail end of winter and firmly ushering in spring. In the garden, swathes of daffodils toss their golden heads above hopeful young lettuce and fast-rising sorrel. Since deer don't like daffodils, I plant them thickly all around the vegetable beds, where they provide early bees with a morning meal. By having something in bloom in every season, we teach the bees to regard our gardens as a haven and a fine restaurant, which helps to ensure that our fruits and vegetables will be well pollinated come summer.

The wild winds of equinoctial March tend to be soft, warm chinooks that scour the garden's every corner, tossing leaves and twigs about by the handful. As soon as you've gathered them up for the compost, the legendary showers of April arrive, ready to wash down anything that's left behind. Wind and rain help degrade natural materials like leaves, needles, and twigs, which slowly release their stored nutrients into the waiting soil as the temperatures begin to rise.

Overleaf: Edible flowers and mesclun mix; yellow globe onions.

Don't wait until it's warm, but spread your compost early, so that by gentle May, when calmer weather arrives, the garden is set for a healthy, productive summer.

When you set out young plants, remember that May's mild temperatures can be deceptive. Until the soil warms up, which can take quite a while, those beds are still pretty chilly. Tropical crops like tomatoes, beans, corn, basil, and cilantro are not happy in chilly Northwestern springs, where cool nights and cool soils combine to slow their growth. Wait until Memorial Day to plant warm-weather crops, or place them in mounded beds with protective row covers. Tomato cages wrapped in row cover cloth will also help conserve warmth (leave the tops open, however).

Early in spring, rhubarb thrusts plump, rosy red shoots through the softening soil. Rhubarb foliage contains toxic compounds not found in the stems, so please don't be tempted to toss the pretty little leaves in a salad. Wait a while and those succulent stems will be long enough to pull for chutney, pie, and cobbler.

As spring matures, the garlic tips and larger onion greens gain a fresh new flavor and a delicious pungency that make them welcome in chicken salad or rice pilaf. Pencil-thin and straight as little arrows, baby spring onions are ready for salads. Harvest them whole and chop them into soups, salads, and side dishes, or slice their root ends lengthwise into frills to make a toothsome garnish for grilled fish or roasted chicken.

Hardy kitchen herbs awaken in spurts as winter departs, stretching and yawning before leafing out with renewed vitality. The elderly parsley that held on bravely all winter looks tattered and worn next to the leafy new shoots that spring up fresh from willing roots. Thyme is covered with tiny new leaves, and sage opens tightly clustered leaves at the tip of each branch.

By midspring, sprigs of fresh marjoram and oregano lend zest to dressings and spring salads. As dill and fennel unfurl feathery foliage, snip some of those ferny fronds for the kitchen. Both bulbing Florence fennel and the perennial, almost shrubby variety offer tasty leaves that refresh salads, sauces, and dressings. Delicate sprigs of fine-textured dill foliage also make a delicious addition to a spring salad. A combination of tiny baby greens and fresh herb sprigs will enliven a plain sandwich or garnish an ordinary soup with grace.

Fresh stalks of rhubarb.

Boost plants' growing power with spring fertilizers

As spring arrives, you can remove cloches and row cover wrappings from winter-planted crops, which leap forward to meet the new season with vigor. Sow all-season lettuces and greens every few weeks through spring. Keep your rows short, 2 to 3 feet or less in length, depending on how many people you need to feed. It's always tempting to overplant in early spring, when we've forgotten how huge these tiny plants will soon be.

Before sowing, work some cottonseed or soy meal into the soil, as well as plenty of compost. Where young plants are growing strongly, offer them a top dressing of aged dairy manure, mature compost, and the large alfalfa pellets used for calf feed (unmedicated, please; plants don't need steroids—which end up in the local water system—and neither do you). This will provide a rush of instant nitrogen as well as a slow feed that will support your hungry plants through their brief lifetime.

Here are my favorite "recipes" for a spring booster fertilizer and an all-purpose feeding mulch.

Spring Booster

4 parts cottonseed or soy meal
1 part dolomite lime (not outhouse lime)
1 part rock phosphate
½ part kelp meal

This recipe is measured by volume, so 1 part may equal 1 cup or 1 bucket. Blend all of the ingredients and add a moderate amount to each planting hole. (Use about 1 tablespoon for a plant from a 4-inch pot.) You can also work in a moderate quantity to a depth of 4 to 6 inches along the row line when sowing seeds.

To feed established plants, gently scratch an appropriate amount into the soil from the plant's crown or trunk to the dripline, then cover with 2 to 4 inches of compost. Use a scant ¼ cup for a gallon-sized transplant, about ½ cup for 5-gallon-sized plants, and a cup or more for large, mature plants, as well as for all rose bushes and clematis, which are gross feeders.

March is also a splendid time to refresh the fruit and vegetable beds with a milder spring feeding mulch that offers a gentle combination of quick and slow-release nutrients that can be used pretty much anywhere in quantity.

All-Purpose Spring Feeding Mulch

2 parts alfalfa pellets (unmedicated calf manna)
1 part aged dairy cow or barnyard manure (bagged is fine)
1 part mature compost

This recipe is also measured by volume, so each part equals 1 bucketful or whatever unit you prefer. Mix it all up in a wheelbarrow and spread the feeding mulch 1 inch deep over planting beds and around existing plants. Store any extra in a trash can with a tight-fitting lid.

This mild feeding mulch will be appreciated by established camellias and rhododendrons, blueberries and cane fruits, fruit trees, and strawberries. The only caution to observe is not to pile it too thickly near any plant's trunk or crown; nobody likes to be smothered by their breakfast.

Encourage soil biota with compost or compost tea

March and April are good times to renew the compost blanket that kept the garden snug all winter. Spread mature compost generously under the daffodils to keep those pretty flowers free of mud splash. Sheet-mulch with compost, spreading it 3 to 4 inches deep, in all the vegetable beds, feathering it to a mere ¼ inch near the crowns of any existing perennials and the trunks of shrubby herbs, and spreading it thickly at the driplines and in any open areas.

Mulching with compost encourages the growth of soil biota, the tiny creatures that bring soil to life. Soil biota include a tremendous quantity and variety of living beings, from protozoa and amoebas to bacteria and fungi, as well as bigger creatures like sowbugs and worms.

Soil biota help transform compost and other nutrients into forms that plants can readily absorb. Thus, if you feed the soil and encourage a healthy crop of beneficial biota, your plants will thrive in turn. Luckily, you don't need to figure out just the right diet for each of the thousands or even millions of critters that may inhabit a mere teaspoon of soil. All you need to do is annually renew your mulch with the best compost you can make or buy, adding moderate amounts of mild natural fertilizers like soy and cottonseed meal right where plants need them—in the root zone.

You may also want to add moderate amounts of agricultural lime to help neutralize acid Northwestern soils, but this isn't needed every year. Having your soil tested every few years and observing how well your plants grow will help you know when it is needed.

If your property is extensive and spreading tons of compost seems arduous, or if you don't have room to make your own compost, there is an excellent alternative. Seek out a local nursery that makes aerobically brewed compost tea, which is a concentrated inoculant of soil biota. These teas are alive, so they must be used the day they are brewed. Instead of spreading compost with a shovel, you can spray the tea with a pressure sprayer. A little goes a long way; a gallon of fresh tea covers about 1,000 square feet.

If repeated monthly or so, a light film of living tea is enough to visibly improve the nature and texture of soil within a few months. Sprayed on plants, brewed teas can help prevent or limit the effects of foliage disorders like black spot, powdery mildew, and rust. Tea sprays also reduce or eliminate molds and mildews on foliage and lawns. They are effective on plants that tend to get botrytis (like peonies) or mosaics (like tomatoes and beans) as well.

The first time you use this tea, or if you are treating a plant with a problem, use it full strength. Don't glug it on; a light misting is still the most efficient way to get good coverage. Use a pressure sprayer or a dairy teat washer to coat the foliage on both top and bottom for best protection.

Once the garden is fed and mulched, you are ready to plant. Most spring planting is done in fits and starts, a bit at a time to stagger the harvesting period. As with lettuce, sow or plant in short rows or patches, spacing plants or thinning seedlings to allow enough room for each plant to take its natural shape without crowding. However, plants are communal by nature and grow best in colonies. Space your plants so the foliage barely touches at maturity, leaving enough of a gap to allow for good air circulation. This natural spacing creates a benign moist zone below the soil's surface that helps encourage the rapid growth of soil biota.

The glory of spring: raised vegetable and herb garden.

spring recipes

entrées

Peppered Pork Loin and New Potatoes
Halibut with Rhubarb and Blood Orange Chutney
Herbed Salmon Steaks with Lemon Herb Sauce
Shrimp and Pea Stir-Fry
Roast Chicken with Spring Vegetables
Hot Chicken Noodle Salad

soups and stews

Corn Chowder with New Potatoes
Fresh Pea Soup with Ginger
Spring Sorrel Soup
Chilled Green Goddess Soup

Flourishing chives.

side dishes

Jasmine Rice with Sugar Snap Peas
Asparagus with Shallot, Thyme, Parsley, and
    Lemon Sauce
Romanesco Broccoli with Tangerine-Walnut Sauce
Broccoli with Creamy Sorrel Sauce
Dandelion Greens and Radicchio with Pancetta
Snappy Kale and Sorrel Stir-Fry

salads

Shrimp and French Sorrel Salad
Lemony Minted Carrot Salad
Fresh Tuna Salad
Arugula Salad with Cherry Chive Vinaigrette
Snow Pea Salad
Herbed Spinach Salad
Asparagus Salad with Creamy Herb Dressing

baked goods and sweets

Herbed Goat Cheese Scones
Rhubarb Brown Betty
Lemon-Ginger Shortcake with Strawberries and
    Lemon-Vanilla Cream
Strawberries and Dipping Cream

spring menus

march

Herbed Salmon Steaks with
Lemon Herb Sauce

Dandelion Greens and Radicchio
with Pancetta

Lemony Minted Carrot Salad

Herbed Goat Cheese Scones

april

Halibut with Rhubarb and
Blood Orange Chutney

Asparagus with Shallot, Thyme, Parsley,
and Lemon Sauce

Jasmine Rice with Sugar Snap Peas

Rhubarb Brown Betty

may

Fresh Pea Soup with Ginger

Roast Chicken with Spring Vegetables

Broccoli with Creamy Sorrel Sauce

Herbed Spinach Salad

Lemon-Ginger Shortcake with
Strawberries and Lemon-Vanilla Cream

entrées

Peppered Pork Loin and New Potatoes

Spring evenings still run cool, though day temperatures are slowly rising. Sweet-hot roasted garlic and meltingly tender new potatoes are a delightful accompaniment for this pepper-crusted pork loin.

Lean pork loin roast, about 1½ pounds
1 tablespoon olive oil
1 teaspoon kosher salt
1 tablespoon peppercorns, cracked (put in
    a bag and crush with a rolling pin)
1 tablespoon fresh rosemary leaves, or ½
    teaspoon dried rosemary
1 teaspoon sliced fresh sage leaves, or ½
    teaspoon dried sage, crumbled
1 whole head garlic, separated and peeled
1½ pounds organic new potatoes, pricked
    with a fork

■ Preheat the oven to 400°F. Rinse the pork, pat it dry, and rub with 1 teaspoon of the olive oil. Sprinkle all over with ½ teaspoon of the salt and the peppercorns, patting to keep them in place.

■ Coat a large baking dish with the remaining 2 teaspoons oil, add the rosemary, sage, and garlic, and roll the potatoes in the oil before sprinkling them with the remaining ½ teaspoon salt. Place the pork in the pan with the potatoes, reduce the heat to 325°F, and bake for 45 to 60 minutes, until potatoes are fork-tender, meat is well browned, and internal temperature is 185°F. Serve warm.

Makes 4 servings

Variegated oregano, sage, and ginger mint.

Halibut with Rhubarb and Blood Orange Chutney

Tart-sweet, ruby red Italian blood oranges add panache to the rhubarb chutney sauce that enlivens this pan-fried halibut fillet. This garlicky sauce is also splendid with all kinds of meat, from turkey or chicken to roast pork or lamb.

2 teaspoons virgin olive oil

2 cloves garlic, chopped

1½ pounds halibut fillet (2 inches thick), cut into 4 pieces

1 bunch cilantro, stemmed, for garnish

Rhubarb and Blood Orange Chutney

1 teaspoon virgin olive oil

2 dried hot red chiles

2 cloves garlic, chopped

1 onion, chopped

¼ teaspoon kosher or sea salt

1 teaspoon ground cumin

½ teaspoon ground coriander

¼ teaspoon ground nutmeg

2 cups diced rhubarb (1-inch pieces)

1 to 3 tablespoons sugar or fructose (see sidebar, page 135)

2 organic blood oranges, sectioned and membrane removed

■ To prepare the Rhubarb and Blood Orange Chutney, in a medium saucepan, heat the 1 teaspoon of olive oil with the chiles over medium-high heat. Brown the chiles well to flavor the oil, then remove and discard them. Add the garlic and onion. Sprinkle with the salt, cumin, coriander, and nutmeg and cook, stirring, until golden, 5 to 7 minutes. Add the rhubarb, cover the pan, reduce heat to medium-low and simmer until tender, about 15 minutes. Add sugar to taste (the mixture should taste sweet-tart). Remove from the heat, stir in the blood orange sections, and set aside.

■ In a frying pan, heat the 2 teaspoons of olive oil and the garlic over medium-high heat. Add the halibut and cook over medium heat until fish is opaque when flaked, 5 to 6 minutes per side. Serve at once, topped with the chutney and garnished with cilantro.

Makes 4 servings

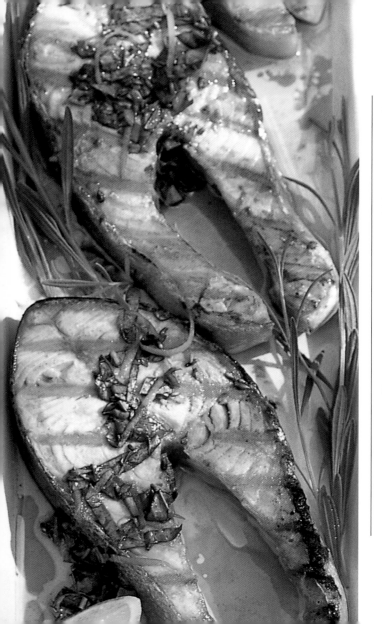

Herbed Salmon Steaks with Lemon Herb Sauce

For an aromatic, smoky finish, add a handful of thyme or rosemary twigs to the coals before grilling your salmon steaks. Assemble the creamy lemon sauce while the fish cooks, or make it ahead (it keeps well overnight in the fridge).

2 pounds salmon steaks
1 tablespoon virgin olive oil
¼ teaspoon kosher or sea salt
½ teaspoon dried red chile flakes
1 teaspoon fresh thyme leaves
1 teaspoon fresh oregano leaves
1 teaspoon fresh marjoram leaves

Lemon Herb Sauce

1 cup sour cream (nonfat works fine)
1 bunch fresh lemon balm leaves, shredded (about ¾ cup)
1 teaspoon fresh lemon thyme leaves
2 to 3 grinds nutmeg
¼ teaspoon kosher or sea salt
Juice and grated zest of 1 organic lemon
1 teaspoon drained green peppercorns

■ Start coals in a grill. Rinse the salmon steaks, pat dry, and set aside. In a shallow bowl, combine the olive oil, salt, chile flakes, thyme, oregano, and marjoram. Dredge the salmon in the oil mixture, coating it on both sides. Grill over medium coals until fish is opaque and flakes easily, 8 to 12 minutes per side, turning once.

■ To prepare the Lemon Herb Sauce, combine the sour cream with the lemon balm, lemon thyme, nutmeg, salt, and lemon zest in a food processor or blender. Process until smooth, and then stir in the green peppercorns. (You can make the sauce ahead and refrigerate it at this stage, leaving the lemon unjuiced.)

■ At serving time, add the lemon juice to the sauce. Drizzle the sauce over the salmon and serve.

MAKES 4 SERVINGS

Shrimp and Pea Stir-Fry

Fast and tasty, this spicy stir-fry combines snow peas and fresh shelled peas. Serve it over rice or fast-cooking rice noodles, and use any leftovers to stuff a brunch omelet. Light and sparkly sanbaizu combines natural brown rice vinegar with soy sauce and sweet rice vinegar.

1 tablespoon vegetable oil
2 or 3 dried hot red chiles or Chinese hot
  peppers
1 clove garlic, chopped
1 onion, chopped
¼ teaspoon kosher or sea salt
2 stalks celery, chopped
1 pound cooked, peeled shrimp
1 cup shelled new peas
1 cup snow peas
2 ounces enoki mushrooms, rinsed and
  drained
1 tablespoon sanbaizu seasoning sauce or
  plum vinegar
1 cup cashews or peanuts, toasted

■ In a wok or frying pan, heat the oil with the dried chiles over medium-high heat. Brown the chiles on all sides to flavor the oil, and then remove and discard the chiles. Add the garlic and onion, sprinkle with the salt, and cook, stirring, until the onion is barely soft, 2 to 3 minutes. Add the celery and shrimp and cook for 1 to 2 minutes. Add the shelled peas and cook for 1 to 2 minutes. Add the snow peas and cook for another 1 to 2 minutes. Add the mushrooms and cook for 1 to 2 minutes longer. Add the sanbaizu or vinegar, cook for 1 minute more, and serve, topped with the toasted nuts.

MAKES 4 SERVINGS

Roast Chicken with Spring Vegetables

When roasted with fennel, asparagus, new potatoes, and lemon balm, plain chicken becomes an aromatic sensory treat. Any leftovers will taste great in a luncheon salad.

1 roasting chicken, 3 to 4 pounds
¼ cup fresh lemon balm leaves
1 tablespoon fresh thyme leaves
2 tablespoons stemmed fresh fennel greens
2 tablespoons olive oil
4 small bulbs Florence fennel, ends trimmed
1 bunch asparagus, ends snapped off
1 pound organic new potatoes, well scrubbed
8 ounces snow peas, ends trimmed
¼ teaspoon kosher or sea salt
1 lemon, cut into quarters, for garnish

■ Preheat the oven to 350°F. Loosen the chicken skin and cover the bird with lemon balm leaves, sliding them under the skin. Use about 3 tablespoons of the leaves. Shred the

Fennel comes in several forms and grows in almost any kind of soil.

remaining lemon balm and combine in a small bowl with the thyme, fennel greens, and olive oil. Brush the fennel, asparagus, potatoes, snow peas, and chicken lightly with the herbed oil and sprinkle with the salt. Place the vegetables and chicken in a roasting pan and roast until chicken is done, about 1 hour. Let rest for 5 minutes. Carve the chicken and serve with the vegetables, spooning pan juices over each portion. Garnish with lemon wedges.

MAKES 4 SERVINGS

cook's tip

both the stalks and the fine-textured foliage of fennel are used in Mediterranean cooking. In spring, Italians eat infant Florence fennel raw, dressed with lovely olive oil. It can be thinly slivered into salads, chopped for soups, steamed, sautéed, stir-fried, or roasted with root vegetables. Florence fennel is also known as bulbing fennel, finocchio, sweet fennel, and annual fennel (see page 93).

Hot Chicken Noodle Salad

When you can spare only half an hour for making dinner, try this hot chicken noodle salad. The savory sour cream sauce is vibrant with fennel and dried apricots. Substitute thin strips of pork if you prefer, and use dried red currants in place of apricots. Both versions are simple yet sumptuous.

8 to 9 ounces fresh noodles
2 tablespoons virgin olive oil
1 dried hot red chile
2 cloves garlic, chopped
1 teaspoon fresh rosemary leaves
2 skinless, boneless chicken breast halves
    (1 whole breast), thinly sliced, or 1
    pound lean boneless pork, thinly sliced
½ teaspoon kosher or sea salt
½ teaspoon freshly ground black pepper
Juice and grated zest of 1 organic orange
2 bulbs sweet fennel, thinly sliced
¼ cup finely chopped dried apricots
2 cups stemmed, shredded chard or kale
2 cups stemmed baby spinach

1 cup sour cream (nonfat works fine)
1 bunch flat Italian parsley, stemmed, for
    garnish

■ Cook the noodles according to the package directions. In a saucepan, heat the olive oil
over medium-high heat. Add the chile, and
brown on all sides to flavor the oil. Remove and
discard the chile. Add the garlic, rosemary, and
chicken. Sprinkle with the salt, ground pepper,
and orange zest and cook, stirring often, until
chicken is opaque, 8 to 10 minutes.

■ Add the fennel, stir to coat, and cook until
fennel is barely soft, 6 to 7 minutes. Add the
apricots, orange juice, chard, and spinach, cover
the pan, reduce the heat to medium-low, and
cook until the greens are lightly wilted. Stir
in the sour cream and heat through, 1 to 2
minutes. Toss with the hot noodles and serve,
garnished with parsley.

MAKES 4 SERVINGS

soups and stews

Corn Chowder with New Potatoes

On a cool spring evening, a hearty soup or stew still hits the spot. To acknowledge the shifting of seasons, this light but satisfying chowder features tender little new potatoes. Use organic potatoes to avoid having to peel away most of the nutrients and because the delicate young skins taste so good.

2 pounds organic new potatoes, cut in half
2 cloves garlic, chopped
1 teaspoon salt
1 tablespoon butter or virgin olive oil
1 small onion, chopped
4 cups milk (nonfat works fine)
2 cups corn kernels (frozen works fine)
½ teaspoon freshly ground black pepper
1 bunch flat Italian parsley, stemmed, for garnish

Start corn from seed indoors, and plant out after soil is warm, in the mid- to high 60s.

■ Put the potatoes, garlic, and ½ teaspoon of the salt in a medium saucepan with water to cover. Bring to a boil over high heat, reduce the heat to medium, and simmer until tender, 12 to 15 minutes. Skim off the foam and set aside.

■ In a large saucepan, melt the butter over medium heat. Add the onion and cook until soft, 5 to 7 minutes. Add the milk and corn and heat through, 10 to 12 minutes. Partially drain the potatoes, reserving the bottom few inches of water with the garlic and potato sludge. Add the potatoes and reserved water to the milk mixture and heat though, 3 to 5 minutes. Add the remaining ½ teaspoon salt and the pepper and serve, garnished with parsley.

MAKES 4 SERVINGS

Fresh Pea Soup with Ginger

Fresh pea soup is totally unlike its thick winter counterpart made from dried peas. Light and fresh tasting, this version is beautiful in the bowl and on the palate. It's also quick and easily made, perfect for a light lunch or to start off a leisurely dinner.

1 tablespoon vegetable oil
2 cloves garlic, chopped
1-inch piece ginger root, peeled and finely chopped
1 white or yellow onion, coarsely chopped
½ teaspoon kosher salt or sea salt
4 cups vegetable broth
3 cups shelled new peas
1 bunch cilantro, stemmed, for garnish

■ In a soup pot, heat the oil over medium-high heat. Add the garlic, ginger root, and onion. Sprinkle with the salt, stir, and cook until onion is barely soft, 2 to 3 minutes. Add the broth and bring to a simmer. Add the peas and cook until barely tender and still bright green, 1 to 2 minutes. Serve at once, garnished with the cilantro.

MAKES 4 SERVINGS

Spring Sorrel Soup

Each spring I invent a new recipe for this refreshingly tart herb. This version combines wild and garden sorrels with leeks and fresh thyme. Wild sorrel has a lovely sour-lemon flavor that can't be beat, but Italian parsley makes a tasty garnish as well.

1 tablespoon virgin olive oil

2 leeks, thinly sliced (white and pale green parts only)

About ½ teaspoon salt

1 teaspoon freshly ground black pepper

1 teaspoon fresh thyme leaves

2 bunches French sorrel, stemmed and shredded (about 6 cups)

6 cups vegetable broth

1 tablespoon butter

¼ cup wild sorrel or flat Italian parsley leaves, for garnish

■ Heat the olive oil in a large saucepan over medium-high heat. Add the leeks, sprinkle with ¼ teaspoon of the salt, the pepper, and the thyme, and cook until tender, about 10 minutes. Reduce heat to low, add the sorrel, cover, and cook until limp, 2 to 3 minutes. Add the broth, adjust the salt to taste, and simmer until warm (do not boil). If a smoother consistency is desired, blend in a food processor until smooth. Serve garnished with wild sorrel or parsley.

Makes 4 servings

cook's tip

Culinary sorrel has been brought to perfection by generations of French gardeners, who patiently selected for the largest, most tender leaves with the best flavor. Sorrel makes a delicious filling for savory omelets, and sorrel soup has a velvety texture and a rich yet tart flavor that makes an exciting counterpoint to fish or fowl.

Sweet marjoram, red-veined French sorrel, summer savory, Thai basil 'Siam Queen', cinnamon and sweet basil.

Chilled Green Goddess Soup

This silken concoction takes just minutes to prepare, especially if you pre-chill the broth. Serve it with hunks of crusty Rosemary Bread (page 35) and a green salad laden with fresh herbs.

4 cups vegetable broth, chilled
1 bunch cilantro, stemmed
1 bunch flat Italian parsley, stemmed
1 bunch spinach, stemmed and shredded
1 avocado, diced
2 cloves garlic, chopped
1 red onion, coarsely chopped
About ½ teaspoon kosher salt or sea salt
About ½ teaspoon freshly ground black pepper
2 tablespoons coarsely grated firm Italian cheese, such as pecorino or Asiago, for garnish

■ In a food processor or blender, combine the chilled broth with the cilantro, parsley, spinach, avocado, garlic, and onion. Process to the desired consistency (chunky or smooth). Add salt and pepper to taste, starting with ¼ teaspoon of each. Serve at once, garnished with grated cheese.

MAKES 4 SERVINGS

side dishes

Jasmine Rice with Sugar Snap Peas

Sizzling with Thai green curry paste, this rice dish is a pleasant entrée for a light brunch. It also makes a splendid side dish for roast chicken or grilled salmon.

1 tablespoon virgin olive oil
2 cloves garlic, chopped
1 cup jasmine rice, rinsed
½ teaspoon kosher or sea salt
¼ cup golden raisins
⅛ teaspoon ground nutmeg
3½ cups vegetable or chicken broth
½ to 1 teaspoon Thai green curry paste

1 pound sugar snap peas, ends trimmed
1 bunch green onions, sliced on the
     diagonal into ½-inch pieces
1 bunch cilantro, stemmed, for garnish

■ In a medium-sized, heavy saucepan, heat the oil. Add the garlic and cook over medium-high heat until lightly browned, 2 to 3 minutes. Stir in the rice and cook, stirring occasionally, until lightly golden, 4 to 6 minutes. Add the salt, raisins, nutmeg, and 3 cups of the broth. Bring to a boil, reduce heat to low, and cook, covered, until done, about 20 minutes. When the rice is done, remove from the heat, fluff with a fork, and set aside.

■ Combine the remaining ½ cup broth and the Thai curry paste in a small saucepan over high heat. When it comes to a boil, add the sugar snap peas and green onions, reduce heat to medium, cover the pan, and cook for 1 minute. Serve at once over the rice, garnished with cilantro.

Makes 4 servings

Asparagus with Shallot, Thyme, Parsley, and Lemon Sauce

The tangy shallot sauce perfectly offsets the rich, sweet flavor of young asparagus. It's great alongside fish or fowl, and can be made with any steamed or roasted vegetable.

2 teaspoons virgin olive oil
2 shallots, thinly sliced
½ teaspoon kosher or sea salt
1 teaspoon fresh lemon thyme leaves, or ½
     teaspoon dried thyme
Juice and grated zest of 1 organic lemon
2 bunches asparagus, tough bottom ends
     snapped off
2 teaspoons butter
1 bunch flat Italian parsley, stemmed
½ teaspoon freshly ground black pepper

■ Heat the olive oil in a frying pan over medium-high heat. Add the shallots, salt, thyme, and lemon zest and cook, stirring, until shallots are pale golden, 3 to 4 minutes. Add the

asparagus, reduce heat to medium, cover, and cook, stirring occasionally, until barely soft, 2 to 3 minutes. Add lemon juice to taste, starting with 2 teaspoons. Place the asparagus on a serving platter.

■ Add the butter to the frying pan, and melt quickly over medium-high heat. Stir in the parsley and pepper, pour the sauce over asparagus, and serve.

MAKES 4 SERVINGS

Asparagus thrives in full sun and well-drained soil.

Romanesco Broccoli with Tangerine-Walnut Sauce

Romanesco broccoli forms handsome florets like little spiraling turrets. Break them off and steam or sauté them, then top them with a sprightly sauce like this one to wake up the subtle sweetness in this broccoli cousin.

1 tablespoon olive oil
1 tablespoon butter
2 shallots, finely chopped
½ teaspoon salt
Juice and grated zest of 1 organic
    tangerine
1 teaspoon fresh tarragon leaves
⅓ cup chopped toasted walnuts
1 head Romanesco broccoli, florets
    trimmed

■ In a small saucepan over medium heat, heat the olive oil with the butter until butter melts. Add the shallots and ¼ teaspoon of the salt. When shallots are golden, stir in the tangerine juice, tangerine zest, tarragon, and walnuts; reduce heat to low.

Organic broccoli 'Romanesco'.

■ Set a vegetable steamer basket in a large saucepan over several inches of water and bring to a boil. Add the Romanesco broccoli florets, sprinkle with the remaining ¼ teaspoon salt, cover, and cook until tender, 3 to 5 minutes. Serve hot, drizzled with the sauce.

MAKES 4 SERVINGS

Broccoli with Creamy Sorrel Sauce

Steam tender organic broccoli lightly, then drizzle it with this fabulous sauce to turn it into a dish worthy of a feast.

cook's tip

among the most popular of vegetables, broccoli is well worth growing at home organically, especially if you are feeding a family. Some years back, *Consumer Reports* reported on foods that retain significantly high levels of pesticide residues. Broccoli and strawberries topped the list.

2 cups broccoli crowns (1 large bunch, stemmed)
1 tablespoon virgin olive oil
2 cloves garlic, minced
¼ teaspoon salt
1 bunch French sorrel, stemmed and shredded
1 cup plain yogurt or sour cream (nonfat works fine)
1 cup fresh cilantro leaves, for garnish

■ Place the broccoli in a steamer basket set in a large saucepan over 2 inches of water. Bring to a boil over medium-high heat and steam until tender, 4 to 6 minutes.

■ While the broccoli cooks, heat the olive oil in a medium saucepan over medium-high heat. Add the garlic and salt and cook, stirring, until garlic is pale golden, 2 to 3 minutes. Add the sorrel, cover, and cook until wilted, 2 to 3 minutes. Stir in the yogurt, cover, and heat through.

■ When broccoli is done, heap it in a serving dish, drizzle with the sauce, and serve at once, garnished with cilantro.

MAKES 4 SERVINGS

Dandelion Greens and Radicchio with Pancetta

When I lived in Italy, an elderly neighbor taught me to sauté dandelion greens and radicchio with lean Italian salt pork and onions. Wow! The bitter bite of radicchio is perfectly offset by the richness of the pancetta. A touch of pepper lends the dish a lively lift.

> 2 cups loosely packed young dandelion greens, stemmed
> 1 teaspoon olive oil
> 1 hot chile
> 1 red or sweet onion, thinly sliced
> ½ teaspoon kosher salt
> 2 strips lean pancetta, chopped
> 1 bunch or 1 bag radicchio (about 2 cups), stemmed
> 1 lemon, cut into wedges, for garnish

■ Rinse the greens and shake lightly, leaving them damp. Set aside.

■ Heat the olive oil in a large saucepan over medium-high heat. Add the chile and sauté until brown on all sides, about 1 minute, to flavor the oil. Remove and discard chile.

■ Add the onion to the oil, stirring to coat. Sprinkle with the salt and sauté until warmed through, 1 to 2 minutes. Add the bacon and cook until crisp, stirring several times, 3 to 4 minutes. Add the greens and radicchio, reduce heat to medium-low, cover, and cook until greens are barely limp, 1 to 2 minutes.

■ Serve at once, garnishing each portion with a lemon wedge. Drizzle with lemon juice and dig in!

MAKES 4 SERVINGS

Snappy Kale and Sorrel Stir-Fry

Spicy with peppers, crunchy with peanuts, and intriguingly savory, this speedy stir-fry of leafy greens makes a delicious accompaniment for grilled fish or chicken.

2 cups loosely packed shredded kale
1 bunch French sorrel, stemmed and
    shredded (about 2 cups)
1 teaspoon vegetable oil
1 teaspoon dark sesame oil
1 hot chile
1 red bell pepper, thinly sliced
2 stalks celery, thinly sliced
1 small onion, thinly sliced
½ teaspoon kosher salt
2 tablespoons Thai sweet chili sauce or
    your favorite stir-fry sauce
¼ cup chopped peanuts or sesame seeds,
    toasted, for garnish

■ Rinse the kale and sorrel and shake lightly, leaving them damp. Heat the vegetable oil and the sesame oil in a large saucepan over medium-high heat. Add the chile and sauté until brown on all sides, about 1 minute, to flavor the oil. Remove and discard the chile. Add the bell pepper, celery, and onion, stirring to coat. Sprinkle with the salt and sauté until barely cooked, 2 to 3 minutes. Add the greens, reduce heat to medium-low, cover, and cook until greens are barely limp, 1 to 2 minutes. Stir in the chili sauce (or whatever sauce you prefer) and serve at once, garnishing each portion with chopped peanuts or sesame seeds.

Makes 4 servings

salads

Shrimp and French Sorrel Salad

This hearty entrée salad combines tangy, lemon-flavored French sorrel with a jumble of shrimp, bacon, and eggs in a snappy curried vinaigrette.

>   2 tablespoons olive oil
>   2 to 3 teaspoons balsamic or rice vinegar
>   6 cups young salad greens
>   1 cup shredded French sorrel leaves
>   4 hard-boiled eggs, cut into wedges
>   4 slices lean peppered bacon, chopped into
>   ¼-inch pieces
>   1 small onion, thinly sliced
>   1½ cups cooked, peeled shrimp
>   1 teaspoon curry powder

■ In a jar, blend the oil and vinegar, shake well, and set aside. Arrange the greens and shredded sorrel on 4 plates, and top with the egg wedges.

■ In a large frying pan, cook the bacon over medium-high heat until crisp and golden, 4 to 6 minutes. Add the onion and cook until barely soft, 2 to 3 minutes. Reduce heat to medium-low, add the shrimp and the curry powder, and heat through, 2 to 3 minutes.

■ Using a slotted spoon, divide the hot bacon and shrimp mixture among the salad plates. Add the balsamic dressing to the frying pan and swirl it to collect all the pan juices. Drizzle the dressing over each salad and serve at once.

MAKES 4 SERVINGS

Lemony Minted Carrot Salad

Bright, vivid flavor contrasts—lively lemon and mellow mint, crunchy walnuts and sweet golden raisins—give this pretty salad a refreshing taste of spring. For a pleasant change, substitute cilantro for the parsley, and thyme or tarragon for the mint.

2 cups peeled, thinly sliced small carrots
   (about 1 pound)
2 tablespoons golden raisins
½ small red onion, chopped
2 tablespoons chopped toasted walnuts
1 cup parsley leaves

Lemon Mint Dressing

2 tablespoons rice vinegar
3 tablespoons virgin olive oil
1 clove garlic, finely chopped
Juice and grated zest of 1 organic lemon
1 tablespoon finely chopped fresh mint
   leaves
¼ teaspoon kosher or sea salt
¼ teaspoon freshly ground black pepper

■ To prepare the Lemon Mint Dressing, combine the vinegar, olive oil, garlic, lemon juice and zest, mint, salt, and pepper in a jar. Shake well to emulsify, and set aside.

■ In a serving bowl, combine the carrots, raisins, red onion, walnuts, and parsley. Toss gently with the dressing and serve.

MAKES 4 TO 6 SERVINGS

Chocolate mint against Euonymus fortunei *'Emerald and Gold'.*

Fresh Tuna Salad

Start with chunks of tuna, pan-seared with fresh ginger; use lots if you love it and less if you aren't sure. The light garlic and rice vinegar dressing sparkles with fresh orange, creamy avocado, and crunchy peanuts. For a complete meal, just add crusty rolls and a glass of dry white wine.

8 cups spring greens

2 cups shredded arugula

1½ pounds fresh tuna fillet, 1½ to 2 inches
thick, cut into 4 pieces

2 tablespoons virgin olive oil

1- to 4-inch piece ginger root, peeled and
finely chopped

2 cloves garlic, chopped

½ teaspoon kosher or sea salt

Juice and grated zest of 1 organic orange

2 tablespoons rice vinegar

1 avocado, diced

1 organic orange, peeled and sectioned,
membrane removed

1 bunch cilantro, stemmed, for garnish

¼ cup toasted peanuts, for garnish

■ Arrange the greens and arugula on 4 dinner plates.

■ Rub the tuna pieces with 2 teaspoons of the olive oil, pat the ginger root firmly into both sides, and set aside.

■ In a jar, blend the remaining oil, the garlic, ⅛ teaspoon of the salt, orange juice and zest, rice vinegar, avocado, and orange sections; shake well and set aside.

■ In a wide, heavy pan, heat the remaining salt over medium-high heat. Add the fish and sear quickly, 1 to 2 minutes per side. Reduce heat to medium, cover the pan, and cook until fish is barely opaque, 5 to 7 minutes.

■ Arrange the fish on the greens, drizzle with the dressing, and serve, garnished with the cilantro and peanuts.

MAKES 4 SERVINGS

Arugula Salad with Cherry-Chive Vinaigrette

Buttery spinach and peppery arugula combine with fresh chives and dried tart cherries in a sparkling dressing that sings in the mouth. Dried cranberries work fine as a substitute for the cherries, and you can use green onions if you don't have chives on hand.

4 cups salad greens
1 cup shredded arugula
2 cups baby spinach, stemmed

Cherry-Chive Vinaigrette

¼ cup virgin olive oil
About 2 tablespoons sweet brown rice vinegar
1 clove garlic, pressed
1 tablespoon finely chopped garlic chives or any chives
¼ teaspoon kosher or sea salt
¼ teaspoon freshly ground black pepper
2 tablespoons dried tart cherries

■ To prepare the Cherry-Chive Vinaigrette, combine all the ingredients except the vinegar in a jar; then add the vinegar to taste, starting with 1 tablespoon. Cap tightly and shake well to emulsify.

■ Place the salad greens, arugula, and spinach in a salad bowl. Drizzle vinaigrette over the greens, toss, and serve.

MAKES 4 SERVINGS

Snow Pea Salad

Crisp textures and vivid flavors make this salad a family favorite. The spunky sweet rice vinegar dressing is enlivened with fresh lime juice and a splash of ginger tamari (I use the savory organic ginger tamari made by Spectrum).

    2 cups shredded bok choy
    2 cups baby salad greens
    1 bunch cilantro, stemmed
    1 cup mung bean sprouts, rinsed and
        drained

    2 stalks celery, thinly sliced
    2 cups snow peas
    1 bunch flat Italian parsley, stemmed
    2 tablespoons sesame seeds, toasted

Dressing

    ½ cup rice vinegar
    2 teaspoons ginger tamari
    1 clove garlic, minced
    Juice and grated zest of 1 organic lime
    2 teaspoons honey
    Few drops dark sesame oil (optional)

■ To prepare the dressing, in a jar, combine the vinegar, tamari, garlic, lime juice and zest, honey, and sesame oil, if using. Shake well and set aside.

■ In a salad bowl, toss together the bok choy, salad greens, cilantro, bean sprouts, and celery. Top with the snow peas, parsley, and sesame seeds. Drizzle with the dressing, and serve at once.

MAKES 4 SERVINGS

Herbed Spinach Salad

For a light lunch, toss young spinach with a generous helping of herbs and fresh vegetables, and dress with a quick sweet rice vinaigrette.

4 cups baby spinach, stemmed
3 cups fresh young greens
1 cup fresh herb sprigs (dill, fennel, thyme, lemon balm, chives)
1 red bell pepper, thinly sliced
1 carrot, peeled and thinly sliced
1 small bulb fennel, thinly sliced
4 green onions, thinly sliced

Dressing

2 tablespoons olive oil
1 teaspoon dark sesame oil
1 tablespoon rice vinegar or mirin (sweet rice wine)

■ Toss the spinach, greens, and herb sprigs together in a large salad bowl and layer the bell pepper, carrot, fennel, and green onions over them.

■ To prepare the dressing, blend the oils and the vinegar in a jar, adjusting the quantities to taste. Drizzle the dressing over the salad and serve at once.

MAKES 4 TO 6 SERVINGS

Left: Golden crinkled oregano, golden variegated sage, Greek oregano, variegated ginger mint. Right: Cuban variegated oregano, marjoram, pineapple sage, nasturtium, and Wedgewood English thyme.

Asparagus Salad with Creamy Herb Dressing

Quickly steam the first slim spears of asparagus, then drizzle them lightly with this tart, tangy blend of sour cream or yogurt, minced garlic, and fresh lemon balm. A touch of lemon thyme gives this dish extra body, but feel free to use orange thyme or even a bit of marjoram if you prefer.

1 pound asparagus, tough ends trimmed
¼ teaspoon salt
4 cups mixed baby greens
2 cups thinly sliced bok choy or Chinese cabbage
4 green onions, thinly sliced
4 mushrooms, thinly sliced
1 tablespoon thinly sliced lemon balm leaves, for garnish

Creamy Herb Dressing

1 cup sour cream or yogurt (nonfat works fine)
2 cloves garlic, minced or pressed
¼ cup thinly sliced lemon balm leaves
1 teaspoon lemon thyme or any thyme leaves
¼ teaspoon salt

■ To prepare the Creamy Herb Dressing, in a small bowl, blend the sour cream, garlic, lemon balm, thyme, and salt. Stir well to blend and set aside to let the flavors mellow.

■ Put the asparagus into a steamer basket set in a large saucepan over 2 inches of water. Sprinkle with the salt. Cover and bring to a boil. Cook until asparagus is barely tender but still crisp, 2 to 3 minutes. Remove steamer from the pan and let the asparagus cool.

■ Arrange the greens and bok choy on 4 plates and top with the asparagus, green onions, and mushrooms. Drizzle with the dressing and garnish with the remaining tablespoon of lemon balm. Serve at once.

MAKES 4 SERVINGS

baked goods and sweets

Herbed Goat Cheese Scones

Light, rich, and crumbly, these warm scones are packed with fresh garden herbs and chunks of creamy goat cheese. For the fullest flavor, look for local fresh goat cheese, perhaps rolled in herbs or cracked peppercorns. Experiment with a handful of whatever herbs your garden offers, from rosemary and thyme to dill and fennel. Even dried lavender is lovely in this recipe!

1 cup unbleached white flour
½ cup whole wheat pastry flour
½ cup oat flour
1 teaspoon sugar
½ teaspoon salt
2 teaspoons baking powder
¼ cup (½ stick) butter, at room temperature
½ cup coarsely crumbled goat cheese
2 teaspoons chopped fresh herb leaves (such as thyme, rosemary, parsley, marjoram, or lemon balm)
1 teaspoon drained green peppercorns
About 1 cup buttermilk

■ Preheat the oven to 425°F. In a medium bowl, sift together the flours, sugar, salt, and baking powder. With your fingers or a pastry cutter, work in the butter until the mixture has the texture of coarse cornmeal. Gently stir in the goat cheese, herbs, and peppercorns. Slowly blend in the buttermilk until you have a soft dough, starting with ¼ cup (you may not need it all).

■ Lightly roll the dough out about ⅓ inch thick. Use a biscuit cutter to cut 3-inch circles. Place on an ungreased baking sheet, allowing an inch of space between the scones. Bake until golden, 10 to 12 minutes.

MAKES 12 SMALL SCONES

Rhubarb Brown Betty

If you love the tart-sweet balance of this satisfying and simple dessert, freeze a bag or two of sliced rhubarb stems so you can enjoy it any time. Fructose will emphasize the fruity quality of rhubarb without excessive sweetness, but sugar may please your palate better.

3 cups fresh bread crumbs
2 tablespoons butter, at room temperature
2 tablespoons walnut or vegetable oil
¼ teaspoon ground nutmeg
¼ teaspoon ground coriander
½ cup brown sugar
8 cups diced rhubarb (1-inch pieces)
1 to 2 cups sugar, or ½ to 1 cup fructose
Juice and grated zest of 1 organic orange
   (see sidebar, page 30)
½ cup chopped walnuts
½ cup chopped hazelnuts

■ Preheat the oven to 350°F. In a food processor or mixing bowl, blend the bread crumbs, butter, oil, nutmeg, coriander, and brown sugar.

■ Line a 2-quart baking dish with one third of the crumb mixture, top with the rhubarb, and sprinkle with sugar or fructose. (Use the lesser amount if you prefer a tart dessert and the greater amount for a sweeter one.) Drizzle with the orange juice and sprinkle with the orange zest.

■ Blend the walnuts and hazelnuts into the remaining two thirds of the crumb mixture and pat over the top of the rhubarb. Bake until golden brown, about 45 minutes. Serve hot.

MAKES 4 TO 6 SERVINGS

Lemon-Ginger Shortcake with Strawberries and Lemon-Vanilla Cream

For a fabulous dessert, layer fresh organic strawberries between lemony ginger shortcakes with whipped cream. Organic strawberries are pesticide free, as is organic cream, which, not surprisingly, tastes like heaven. Fructose intensifies natural fruit flavors better than white sugars, but it won't do much for cream or baked goods.

2 to 3 cups organic strawberries, hulled
    and sliced
1 to 2 teaspoons fructose or sugar

Lemon-Ginger Shortcake

1 cup plus ¼ cup unbleached white flour
1 cup whole wheat pastry flour
2 teaspoons baking powder
½ teaspoon salt
1 tablespoon sugar
Juice and grated zest of 1 organic lemon
2 tablespoons finely chopped crystallized
    ginger

¼ cup (½ stick) butter (for shorter dough,
    use ½ cup)
⅓ to ½ cup milk (nonfat works fine)

Lemon-Vanilla Cream

1 cup organic heavy cream or whipping
    cream
2 to 3 teaspoons sugar
About 1 teaspoon grated lemon zest
About 1 teaspoon vanilla extract

■ Place the strawberries in a medium bowl, sprinkle with the fructose or sugar, and set aside.

■ To prepare the shortcake, preheat the oven to 450°F. In a medium bowl, sift together the flours, baking powder, salt, and sugar. Add the lemon zest and crystallized ginger. Work in the butter, using your fingers, until no piece is larger than a split pea. Add the lemon juice gradually, starting with 1 tablespoon and increasing by tablespoons. Add the milk in the same manner, using enough to make a barely sticky dough. Sprinkle flour on a work surface, divide the dough into 4 pieces, and pat them out into rounds that are about 1 inch thick. Set them well apart on an ungreased baking sheet and bake until puffed and golden, 10 to 12 minutes. Let cool for 5 minutes on a rack, then split with a fork.

■ To prepare the Lemon-Vanilla Cream, just before serving, whip the cream to soft peaks, adding sugar and vanilla to taste; fold in the lemon zest. Top each shortcake half with strawberries and cream.

MAKES 4 SERVINGS

Strawberries and Dipping Cream

Simple yet sumptuous, this breezy little recipe tastes incredibly sophisticated and will crown any meal with pure gold.

> 1 cup sour cream (nonfat works fine)
> 2 tablespoons brown sugar
> 2 or 3 grinds nutmeg
> 2 cups organic strawberries, lightly rinsed

■ In a small bowl, combine the sour cream, brown sugar, and nutmeg. Arrange the strawberries on a platter and serve with the dip.

MAKES 1 OR 2 SERVINGS

Living fence hoops among strawberry plants.

spring gardening calendar

what to plant	Asparagus, beets, broccoli, Brussels sprouts, cabbage, carrots, cauliflower, collards, fennel, garlic, green onions, kale, lettuce, mustard greens, peas, radishes, rhubarb, shallots, snow peas, spinach, strawberries, Swiss chard, turnips
what to harvest	Asparagus, dandelion greens, garlic greens, green onions, fennel tips, peas, pea vines, kale, radishes, rhubarb, sorrel, young spinach, Swiss chard
what's in the market	Artichokes, asparagus, carrots, lettuce, green onions, kale, mustard greens, peas, radishes, rhubarb, snow peas, spinach, Swiss chard

gardening notes for spring ingredients

■ *Asparagus* This statuesque vegetable requires a lot of space, but both the ferny, filmy foliage and the plump, succulent spring shoots are worth finding room for. Asparagus requires full sun and well-drained soil to thrive. In spring or fall, set young plants in deep garden soil enriched with generous quantities of compost. In clay soils, mounded or raised beds are traditionally used to give asparagus the proper depth of soil.

To promote deep roots and long, plump shoots, plant asparagus in a trench. Scoop the soil away before planting, creating a trench 8 to 10 inches deep. Space plants 12 to 15 inches apart, spreading the roots gently as you plant, and cover with a few inches of soil. As the shoots emerge, carefully add more soil each week or so until the trench is filled in (always leave the shoot tips uncovered).

Let young plants grow for a full year before harvesting any shoots. Next spring, harvest the first shoots when they are 6 to 8 inches long, cutting them cleanly at the base. You may be able to harvest for 2 to 3 weeks the first year, and for as much as 10 weeks with mature plants. When the new shoots that emerge are pencil-thin, stop cutting and let the plants regain strength.

Feed asparagus each spring with booster mulch (see page 54), and use a feeding mulch in early spring or late winter as well. Water asparagus well in dry years to keep the roots growing strongly. Leave the feathery foliage in place until late winter, when the young shoots emerge.

Although you can grow asparagus from seed, you'll have more uniform results with root divisions. Look for plump, crisp roots at least the size of a tennis ball. Mulch mature plants deeply (3 to 4 inches) with compost each fall or spring to conserve moisture and suppress competitive weeds.

Broccoli 'Everest'.

■ *Broccoli* The broccoli clan is extremely popular in Italy, where you can find many kinds of broccoli, including turreted heads of Romanesco broccoli and slim spears of broccolini, as well as green, white, and purple sprouting broccoli and an odd little critter called broccoli raab. All of them thrive in the Northwest, and in mild winters the hardiest forms can be harvested all year round.

Broccoli appreciates a lot of humus and, where soils are heavy, does best in mounded beds. Mulch with compost to reduce problems with rots and molds, and rotate all crucifer-family crops (which includes cabbages, cauliflowers, and Brussels sprouts) to avoid pest and disease issues.

Sow broccoli in short rows from late winter through early spring under cover, and again in staggered late-summer plantings. For the most vigorous root systems, sow into flats or small pots and transplant into the garden.

If you grow broccoli from seed, look for season-extending choices. Open-pollinated forms like 'Waltham' will crop over a longer period than fancy new hybrids that are bred for commercial growers. Winter-sprouting broccoli is very cold hardy and can be sown in both late winter (under cover) and early spring as well as in the fall.

Among the very best open-pollinated broccolis are the pretty red 'Rosalind' and 'Umpqua', both of which produce lots of side shoots that can be harvested over a long period. A newer hybrid called 'Liberty' is productive, tasty, and

beautiful, while the spiky Italian types called 'Romanesco' and 'Minaret' offer tender spears tipped with decorative and delicious rosettes. For tender broccoli raab, consider fast-maturing 'Sorrento' or the tender, tasty 'Zamboni'.

■ *Dandelion Greens* Gardeners are often surprised to learn that dandelion greens are available from seed in named varieties, selected for superior flavor and tenderness. Most of these culinary forms are French or Italian, for Europeans value these humble field greens highly as invigorating spring tonic or "cleansing" greens.

You can harvest your own dandelion greens at home, as long as you avoid any plants that may have been treated with lawn weed and feed or other herbicide products. These systemic toxins can be quite persistent, so stick to dandelions growing in "wild" or organic garden areas.

To gather wild dandelion greens, trim the tops from young plants. Rinse the leaves, trim off any root, and steam, sauté, or stir-fry the greens. The smallest, most tender young leaves can be shredded raw into salads or used as a garnish for grilled fish.

■ *Elephant Garlic* Spring is a fine time to enjoy the last of your garlic crop, which may be sprouting green tips. If so, you can simply snip them for garnish or add them to soups and salads. You can also plant sprouted garlic cloves back into the garden. In my raised beds, the eager garlic starts growing almost immediately. By planting staggered crops in spring and fall, you can pick fresh garlic over a longer period.

Elephant garlic is a lot bigger than regular garlic, with a milder, almost sweet flavor that some folks prefer. When roasted, the sweetness is even more pronounced, making it a great addition to tomato-based pasta sauces that can taste a bit bitter. (See also Garlic, page 43.)

■ *Fennel* Bold, beautiful fennel comes in several forms; the perennial culinary fennel grown for edible foliage and seeds also has several handsome ornamental forms with bronze or reddish foliage. In spring, sow or plant young fennel along a fence or at the back of the garden, where it can stretch to its full 4 to 6 feet in height. Full sun is its only requirement; fennel grows in any kind of soil, though it will be larger and fuller in heavy soils than in sandy ones. One or two plants are enough for most households, and this

abundant self-sower will reproduce gladly and indefinitely.

The seeds of perennial fennel are toasted and used in curries and spice blends and make a pleasantly anise-flavored garnish for salads and vegetable dishes. The fluffy foliage tastes a bit like licorice and can be added in moderate amounts to salads, soups, omelets, and sandwiches.

Annual or bulbing fennel is grown for the tender, plump stalks that make a bulblike swelling at the base of the plant. Also called Florence fennel or finocchio, bulbing fennel is a fast-growing annual that can be sown in late winter (under cover) or in early to late spring. Sow short rows in full sun and in well-drained, compost-enriched soil to lengthen the harvest period. If your soil is heavy, sow Florence fennel in mounded beds for better drainage. To harvest, pull the whole plant and trim off the roots and top growth.

■ *French Sorrel* Kitchen or French sorrel is an easy-to-please leafy perennial herb that is a sophisticated garden cousin of the sour wild sorrel we pull from garden beds. Both owe their tart bite to oxalic acid, which also lends a lemony taste to our native wood sorrel. Though not

Red-veined French sorrel.

botanically related, they share the common name of sorrel as well as a lively flavor.

French sorrel appreciates heavy, acid soils and grows with ease in beds or containers. Best planted in spring or fall; give it a sunny spot well amended with compost, and space the plants generously (18 inches to 2 feet apart) to allow for their natural expansion over the years. Sorrel can often be gathered in small amounts through mild winters and is among the earliest herbs to reappear in spring.

If you can't find starter plants at the local nursery, sorrel is easy to grow from seed. Selected garden forms such as 'Silver Shield' have lovely, marbled leaves that earn room in an ornamental perennial border or a vegetable bed.

■ *Ginger* Ginger is only borderline hardy in the maritime Northwest, where the roots are apt to rot in heavy soils and wet winters, but it grows well in USDA zone 9, especially where nights are warm. Ginger also grows happily in tubs or big, shallow pots and, if brought indoors to a sunroom or heated greenhouse for the winter, can persist for years.

Start your own ginger plants any time of year from fresh roots bought at the grocery store, preferably from an organic source. To sprout the roots, slice them into chunks, making sure each has a rounded bud point (you can see them quite well if you look). Once the cuts seal over (it takes a few days), plant your pieces bud side up in good potting soil, well amended with mature compost.

Keep young plants moist but not soggy, letting them dry out slightly between waterings. Once the leaves appear, ginger appreciates regular watering and may even flower a little in a warm summer. In late fall, ginger foliage will brown off naturally. Back off on watering through the winter until you see fresh growth appearing. Ginger roots can be harvested within 3 to 5 months after planting.

■ *Parsley* This traditional culinary herb grows happily in the Northwest and always winters over in mild years. Flat Italian parsley has a fuller, deeper flavor than the mild-flavored curly-leafed types, which make the prettiest garnish. Sow seed or set out young plants in late winter (under cover) or in early spring. Soak parsley seed for a few hours in cool water before sowing. Sow in flats or pots or right where you want it to grow (it transplants readily when young).

Parsley adapts to most soils but grows best in well-drained soil amended with compost. Harvest the outer leaves as soon as the plants are about 8 to 12 inches tall. Always remove less than you leave to encourage continuing growth. Overwatering results in poor flavor, so let parsley dry out between waterings, and don't water older plants at all.

■ *Rhubarb* Sow seed or set out plants of culinary rhubarbs in late winter (under cover) or early spring. Well-drained soil amended with ample compost helps young rhubarb plants size up quickly. A generous compost mulch helps conserve moisture, which speeds the establishment of young plants, so don't let them dry out completely between waterings. Mature plants are very drought tolerant and long lived.

Give youngsters a year or two of growth before harvesting any of the stalks. When you harvest, pull the stems rather than cutting them to avoid root rots. Always remove less than you leave, even on mature plants, to encourage regrowth.

Among the most beautiful of edible plants, rhubarb comes in a number of ornamental forms as well as the common culinary varieties. The huge leaves of all rhubarbs contain toxins, so never use them as food.

■ *Shelling Peas* Like edible-podded peas, shelling peas are cool-season crops that can be grown in both spring and fall in the maritime Northwest. Shelling peas have tough, inedible pods filled with peas that are generally most succulent when young. Sow shelling peas in early to midspring (St. Patrick's Day is a traditional pea sowing date) and again in staggered fall plantings, sowing in flats, pots, or right where you want them.

Grow shelling peas exactly as you would grow edible-podded peas, allowing plenty of air space between plants. Avoid handling or moving among pea plants when they are wet, which can encourage mildews and molds. Compost mulch helps reduce diseases and can improve the flavor of the peas considerably.

Harvest shelling peas as soon as they are the size you like to eat. Tiny new peas are intensely sweet, while overly mature peas can taste mealy.

Young shelling peas are delicious raw or cooked and can be added to salads, soups, and stir-fries or used in side dishes. Shelling-pea vines and tendrils are also edible and quite tasty when young.

■ *Snow Peas and Sugar Peas* Edible-podded peas are cool-season crops that do very well in the maritime Northwest. Sow edible-podded peas in late winter (under cover) or in early to midspring, and again in staggered fall plantings, sowing in flats, pots, or right where you want them. Young peas transplant readily, and young starts can be set out as soon as you find them in the nurseries in spring and fall. Plant young peas in a sunny place in well-drained soil generously amended and mulched with mature compost. Water them well, and don't let them dry out completely between waterings.

Before planting, soak peas in cool water for a few hours, then roll them in a pea and bean inoculant powder (Territorial Seeds sells a great one) to help them fix nitrogen faster in cold soils. Legume inoculant powder is a stabilized form of rhizobial bacteria that symbiotically assists legume plants to absorb nitrogen from the air and store it in their roots, where it appears as little nodules. Amending and mulching the soil with plenty of compost helps peas get off to a good start and also sustains them in the long run.

Space edible-podded peas 6 to 8 inches apart and provide netting or trellis panels for the tall varieties to climb. Bush peas can be spaced 8 to 12 inches apart. Wide spacing helps increase air circulation and reduces pea enation, early wilts, and mildews. Harvest snow peas as soon as they reach 2 to 3 inches in length, and use them pod and all. Sugar peas can also be eaten as immature pods, eaten pod and all with mature peas inside, or shelled to eat the peas only. Both snow and sugar peas are delicious raw or cooked and can be added to salads, soups, and stir-fries, as can crunchy, delicately flavored tendrils of pea vines (especially the tender tips).

■ *Spinach* A cool-season crop, spinach thrives in the maritime Northwest, where cool nights can greatly prolong the spring harvesting season. Sow spinach weekly in late winter, under cover, in early to midspring, in late summer, and through fall for almost continual cropping.

Sow short rows in a sunny place, in well-drained soil that has been enriched generously with compost and alfalfa meal or pellets. Thin seedlings for salads, leaving room for the

remaining plants to size up (the eventual spacing will be 6 to 8 inches apart). Mulch with 2 to 3 inches of mature compost to conserve moisture, and interplant with sweet alyssum to reduce leaf miner attacks. Spinach grows best with consistent moisture, so don't let it dry out completely between waterings.

Harvest the outer leaves first, and remove less than you leave to encourage continual growth. As summer arrives, pull plants that threaten to bolt (grow tall and spindly and produce flowers). In warmer weather, plant New Zealand spinach or Malabar spinach. Neither is a true spinach, but both taste pretty similar and enjoy warm temperatures.

■ *Strawberries* Strawberries grow best in well-drained soil with lots of compost worked in. Where soils are heavy, mounded beds work best. These low-growing plants are appealing to slugs, so bait with a safe, iron phosphate–based bait such as Sluggo to keep slugs and snails at bay. Don't broadcast the stuff, but tuck a few pellets next to each plant. Keep weeds controlled with compost mulch, being sure not to smother the strawberry crowns when you spread it.

Plant strawberries in spring or fall, placing the plants 12 to 18 inches apart, depending on their size and vigor. Make a small trench 2 to 3 inches deep, and place the plants carefully, spreading the roots gently. Fill the trench with soil, making sure that the strawberry crowns are at soil level (not covered with soil) and that the roots are well covered.

Give strawberries a light feeding mulch in spring (see page 55), followed by a booster feed (see page 54) after harvest.

Most strawberries are colonizing plants. Each mother will send out long stems, each tipped with a tiny baby plantlet that will root wherever it touches ground. To keep a strawberry patch orderly, many growers reset the babies in their own row to grow on to productive size. When the original plants are old and woody, they can be discarded and the youngsters will take over.

Alpine strawberries are small, delicate plants that produce tiny, utterly fabulous berries. June-bearers crop in early summer, while ever-bearers produce most heavily in late spring and early summer but continue sporadically into fall.

Mignonette alpine strawberry.

summer | *june july august*

Summer is an enchanting season

in the garden, from the sweet-scented mornings and lingering twilights of June to the caressing, penetrating warmth of a sultry August afternoon. In June, the garden gates open wide as salads greens mingle with early peas, late asparagus and rhubarb, early strawberries, baby carrots, and the first tiny artichokes. July adds more bounty, with early tomatoes, blueberries and raspberries, sugar peas and tender flageolet beans, zucchini and the first summer squash. By August, there is a positive flood of produce as corn and beans ripen with onions and eggplants, peppers and fat slicing tomatoes, bushels of basil and fluted pattypan squash. Cherries and peaches join the late-cropping strawberries, raspberries, blackberries, and blueberries.

Share the garden bounty

In many gardens, keeping up with this outpouring of abundance can be challenging. One great way to cope is through a giving program. In these difficult economic times, nearly every community has a food bank that serves an increasingly large and diverse population. Why not share your garden's excess produce with people who will be deeply grateful for fresh, wholesome food? Even those out-of-control zucchini will be welcome, as will bags of beans, boxes of tomatoes, and sacks of potatoes. Little bundles of fresh herbs and flowers will brighten somebody's life in an almost effortless way.

To find the food bank nearest you, consult the Yellow Pages of your phone book. You could also contact the nearest social service agency to learn where food donations will be useful and valued.

How do you share the bounty? Wash your extra produce, pack it as appropriate in bags, boxes, or bundles, and label each so the food bank volunteers know what to do with it. Unusual herbs and vegetables are always snapped up quickly in areas with large and varied immigrant populations. Highly perishable produce like lettuce and fresh berries can spoil quickly in summer heat, so unless you know the food bank's schedule, always call ahead to be sure somebody will be on hand to receive your offerings.

Overleaf: Harvest of 'Redbor' kale, Romano and Helda beans, 'Bright Lights' chard, and more; sauce tomatoes.
Right: Potting shed and vegetable and fruit beds.

Handle summer pests and diseases

By summer, there is little to do in a well-mulched vegetable garden but water and harvest crops. If you have a lot of weeds, try using thicker mulches of compost and well-composted, weed-free dairy manure. If you find pests and diseases in your garden paradise, find a local nursery that makes aerobically brewed compost tea. As I discussed in the Spring section, aerobic teas help protect plants against a wide range of diseases, from black spot and downy mildew to sooty mold and rust.

A number of other simple organic solutions are also useful in the vegetable patch. For instance, to stop powdery mildews on the squash family, spray stems and leaves with buttermilk diluted half and half with water. To keep aphids away from your broccoli, cabbages, and other crops, plant "catch crops" of nasturtiums. The aphids will inhabit the nasturtiums by preference, leaving the vegetables unharmed.

If bugs do bug your crops, let your first response be a good, hard stream of water. This may be enough to eliminate some insects, often including aphids, spit bugs, and whiteflies. Where water pressure is low, cover part of the hose outlet with your thumb to reduce the flow and increase the

Plant moisture-loving blueberries in full sun.

pressure. You can also buy an inexpensive attachment called a Bug Blaster that creates a disc of high-pressure water that cleans pests and some diseases off plants without harming the plant.

More stubborn infestations may require a blast with an insecticidal soap. These garden soaps are specially formulated to reduce insect and some disease populations without burning plants. Don't try to use dish or hand soap; it is not the same and may do more harm than good.

For pestier pests, neem tree oil can be a safe yet very effective treatment. In India, parts of the neem tree are used for all sorts of things, from bacteriostatic toothpaste to cosmetics, as well as pesticides and fungicides. Neem oil is a smothering agent that works well against soft-bodied insects, from some caterpillars to aphids and whiteflies, as well as insect eggs and egg cases. It is also useful with certain disfiguring foliage diseases such as molds and mildews.

Wash your harvest

It is very tempting to wander through the garden on a soft summer day, happily nibbling on tomatoes, baby carrots, and tender young beans. However, if water is not on tap in the garden, carry a bowl of warm water with you and at least rinse everything well before you eat it. Better yet, carefully wash everything you plan to eat before you start cooking, including fresh herbs.

'Dusky' eggplant.

Even organically grown produce should be washed carefully after harvest. Many simple organic solutions like neem oil and insecticidal soap are listed as safe for use up to the day of harvest. Even so, it is always best to wash and rinse everything you eat to avoid taking in pesticide or manure residues. Store-bought produce should also be washed in the same way. If you buy produce that is not organically grown, wash it and then soak it for at least 10 minutes in warm water before rinsing to remove as much of the pesticide residues as possible.

This is especially important for children, who are more vulnerable than adults. A recent study in Seattle found indications of pesticide exposure in all but one child among groups of young children (5 to 6 years old) from rural and urban as well as high- and low-income neighborhoods. It turned out that the single pesticide-free child had always been fed organic food and the parents used only natural care products in the home and garden. A follow-up study confirmed that children fed organic food and protected from direct exposure to agricultural and household toxins did indeed tend to be free of detectable pesticide residues.

A Redmond, Washington, vegetable garden at the height of summer.

Purchase a share in a local farm

If your yard is too small to grow a lot of food, consider purchasing a CSA share. CSA, short for Community Supported Agriculture, is rapidly spreading throughout the country. It represents a partnership between growers and consumers who pay farmers in late winter for fruit and vegetables they will receive in summer. These programs vary a great deal, but typically a family might pay $300 to $500 for a 20-week season of produce. One share is usually ample for several people, and half shares are often available for single folks and twosomes.

To find a CSA near you, call your county agricultural extension agent and ask for a list of contacts. This isn't something that's limited to rural or agricultural areas; there's even an extension service office in New York City, as well as thriving farmer's markets in almost every community nationwide. Farmer's markets are great places to find CSA farmers. Look for booths with CSA flyers describing their services, or ask around until you find somebody who can put you in touch with a CSA farmer.

summer recipes

entrées

Pork Medallions with Blueberries and Ginger
Fresh Albacore Tuna with Tomatillo and Sweet Corn
    Salsa
Salmon with Shiso
Salmon with Peach-Raspberry Chutney
Grilled Salmon with Lavender and Basil
Corn and Crab Cakes
Fresh Tomato Pie

soups and stews

Cucumber and Avocado Soup
Cress and Fennel Soup
Summery Onion Soup

side dishes

Dilly Summer Vegetable Mixed Grill
Stuffed Cherry Tomatoes
Stir-Fried Asian Greens and Pea Vines
Margarita Sweet Corn
Grilled Ancho, Sweet Onion, and Corn Salsa

salads

Edible Flower Salad
Prawn Salad with Strawberries and Nectarines
Crisp Chicken Salad with Chipotle Cream Dressing
Insalata di Fagioli e Tonno (Italian Tuna Salad)
Carrot-Marigold Salad
Tomato and Nasturtium Salad with Basil Dressing
Fresh Corn Salad with Sweet Chili–Lime Dressing
Red, White, and Blueberry Salad with Fireworks
    Dressing
Summer Coleslaw with Fresh Tomatillo Salsa
Carrots with Raspberry Purée

baked goods and sweets

Cherries with Fresh Fruit Dipping Sauce
Lemon Sorbet with Huckleberry Sauce
Raspberry-Blueberry Rollups
Italian Baked Peaches with Peach Whipped Cream
Huckleberry-Hazelnut Upside-Down Cake
Summer Garden Shake

'Frost' peaches.

summer menus

june
Cucumber and Avocado Soup

Salmon with Shiso

Edible Flower Salad

Stir-Fried Asian Greens and Pea Vines

Summer Garden Shake

july
Cress and Fennel Soup

Corn and Crab Cakes

Red, White, and Blueberry Salad with
Fireworks Dressing

Margarita Sweet Corn

Lemon Sorbet with Huckleberry Sauce

Lavender Lemonade

august
Fresh Tomato Pie

Insalata di Fagioli e Tonno
(Italian Tuna Salad)

Summer Coleslaw with Fresh
Tomatillo Salsa

Huckleberry-Hazelnut
Upside-Down Cake

entrées

Pork Medallions with Blueberries and Ginger

Snappy with ginger and Japanese chili sauce, this mix of tender pork and tart-sweet blueberries is a winner.

3 teaspoons vegetable oil
2 cloves garlic, minced or pressed
1 cup jasmine rice, rinsed
1 teaspoon kosher or sea salt
Juice and grated zest of ½ organic lemon (cut the other half into 4 wedges, for garnish)
4 lean pork medallions or boneless pork chops (about 1½ pounds)
1- to 2-inch piece ginger root, peeled and chopped
1 onion, thinly sliced
1 red or yellow bell pepper, thinly sliced
1 cup shredded bok choy or joi choy
1 cup blueberries
1 tablespoon rice vinegar
2 to 3 teaspoons Japanese chili sauce or fermented black bean sauce
1 teaspoon sesame seeds, toasted

■ In a medium saucepan, heat 1 teaspoon of the oil over medium-high heat. Add the garlic, rice, ½ teaspoon of the salt, and the lemon zest and toast until golden, 2 to 3 minutes. Measure the lemon juice and add water to make 2 cups. Add to the rice, bring to a boil, reduce heat to low, cover, and simmer until tender, about 20 minutes. When rice is done, remove it from the heat, fluff with a fork, and set aside.

■ Heat the remaining 2 teaspoons oil in a wok or frying pan over medium-high heat. Add the pork medallions and stir-fry until browned, about 5 minutes. Add the ginger root to the wok and stir-fry for 2 minutes. Add the bell pepper and stir-fry for 1 minute. Add the bok choy and stir-fry for 1 minute more. Add the blueberries and stir-fry for another minute. Add the rice vinegar and chili sauce to taste. Serve at once over the rice and garnish with lemon wedges.

MAKES 4 SERVINGS

Fresh Albacore Tuna with Tomatillo and Sweet Corn Salsa

The peppers really make this handsome dish outstanding, so play freely, pairing hot and sweet types. A mixture of jalapeño, such as 'Fiery Festival', 'Hungarian Sweet', and 'Gypsy Sweet', is exceptionally good. Use disposable surgical gloves when handling chiles, or wash your hands with extreme care afterward.

1½ pounds thick albacore tuna fillet
2 cloves garlic, chopped
1 cup plain yogurt or sour cream (nonfat works fine)

Tomatillo and Sweet Corn Salsa

1 teaspoon olive oil
1 cup chopped husked tomatillos
3 or 4 mixed chiles, seeded and chopped
1 sweet onion, chopped
Kernels from 2 ears ripe sweet corn
2 large, ripe tomatoes, chopped
1 bunch fresh cilantro, stemmed

■ Preheat the oven to 325°F. Rinse the fish, pat it dry, and place in a glass baking dish. Add the garlic to the yogurt and spread over the tuna, covering it completely. Bake until the fish is opaque when flaked, 20 to 30 minutes, depending on thickness.

■ To prepare the Tomatillo and Sweet Corn Salsa, heat the oil in a large frying pan over medium heat. Add the tomatillos and chiles and cook, stirring often, until the vegetables are barely soft, 2 to 3 minutes. Add the onion, corn, and tomatoes and cook until barely heated through, 1 to 2 minutes. Remove from heat and stir in the cilantro.

■ Slice the tuna into four pieces and serve with a generous dollop of the corn salsa.

MAKES 4 SERVINGS

Salmon with Shiso

Slightly bitter greens such as shiso (leaf mustard) make a zippy accompaniment to tender salmon. If you don't have any mirin (sweet rice wine), try lemon juice or balsamic vinegar. Each contributes a very distinctive flavor, but all taste good. You can also substitute sturdy halibut in this recipe, if you prefer.

1⅓ cups brown basmati rice or any rice
1½ pounds salmon steaks
½ teaspoon kosher salt, sea salt, or other salt
1 small Walla Walla Sweet onion or red Bermuda onion, thinly sliced
1 teaspoon soy oil
Few drops dark sesame oil (optional)
2 tablespoons mirin (sweet rice wine) or lemon juice
1 bunch red shiso, or any mustard greens, torn
1 small head napa cabbage or bok choy, coarsely chopped
2 or 3 leaves arugula or radicchio, torn into bite-sized pieces
2 or 3 leaves young kale, shredded
¼ teaspoon shoyu (soy sauce), or to taste

■ Cook the rice according to directions on the package.

■ Rinse the fish, and pat it dry. Heat the salt in a large, deep frying pan over medium-high heat. When the salt is hot, add the onion and dry-fry for 1 to 2 minutes to release the juices, stirring occasionally. Add the soy and sesame oils, heat through, and add the fish and mirin. Cover and cook over medium-low heat until the fish flakes easily and is opaque, 10 to 15 minutes.

■ When the fish is done, spoon the warm rice onto a serving platter, add the fish, and cover to retain the heat. Add the shiso to the fish pan and cook over medium-high heat for 2 to 3 minutes. Add the cabbage, arugula, and kale and stir-fry for 1 to 2 minutes. Season to taste with shoyu. Serve the greens over the fish and warm rice.

MAKES 4 SERVINGS

Salmon with Peach-Raspberry Chutney

Next time you have company, try serving this grilled salmon. The Peach-Raspberry Chutney is lively with chile and ginger, soothing with mint, and sparkling with cilantro, for a tart-sweet balance that is both intriguing on the palate and pretty on the plate.

1½ pounds salmon fillet
1 teaspoon virgin olive oil
1 clove garlic, minced
⅛ teaspoon kosher or sea salt

Peach-Raspberry Chutney

1 ripe peach, peeled and chopped
1 cup raspberries
1 Walla Walla Sweet onion, chopped
½-inch piece ginger root, peeled and finely chopped
1 or 2 fresh chile peppers, seeded and chopped
⅓ cup rice vinegar
Juice and grated zest of ½ organic lime
¼ cup cilantro leaves
¼ cup shredded mint leaves
2 cloves garlic, minced
⅛ teaspoon kosher or sea salt

■ Start coals in a grill or preheat the broiler. Rinse the fish, and pat it dry. Rub the skinless side with the olive oil and spread with the garlic and salt.

■ To prepare the Peach-Raspberry Chutney, in a medium bowl, combine the peach, raspberries, onion, ginger, chiles, rice vinegar, lime juice and zest, cilantro, mint, garlic, and salt. Toss gently and set aside.

■ Grill or broil the fish for 3 to 5 minutes per side, turning once. Remove to a plate, cover tightly with foil, and let stand for 5 minutes. Skin the fish and serve with the chutney.

Makes 4 servings

Spicy Thai basil and chives.

Grilled Salmon with Lavender and Basil

This outstanding treat was inspired by the extraordinary food cooked at Purple Haze Lavender Farm in Sequim, Washington. To get leftovers for salads and omelets, double the recipe and dine alone.

> Juice and grated zest of ½ organic lemon (cut the other half into 4 wedges)
> ¼ cup fruity olive oil
> 1 tablespoon shoyu (soy sauce) or tamari
> ¼ cup shredded large-leaf (Genovese type) basil
> 1 teaspoon fresh or dried lavender
> 4 salmon steaks, about 2 pounds total

■ Combine the lemon juice and zest, olive oil, soy sauce, basil, and lavender in a large, resealable plastic bag. Shake well to blend, then add the salmon and gently squeeze the bag to cover the fish with the marinade. Marinate at least an hour or overnight in the refrigerator. Grill or broil the fish for 4 to 6 minutes per side, basting each side twice with marinade. Serve at once, garnished with lemon wedges.

MAKES 4 TO 6 SERVINGS

Lavender Lemonade

a chilled glass of this fragrant and tart-sweet lemonade tastes so cooling on hot summer days.

1 tablespoon fresh or dried lavender florets
4 cups lemonade
4 sprigs mint, for garnish
1 organic lemon, thinly sliced, for garnish

Put the lavender in a small saucepan, pour 1 cup boiling water over it, cover, and let steep for 20 minutes. Strain (a tea strainer works great) and add to the lemonade. Pour into glasses over ice, garnishing each with a mint sprig and a lemon slice.

MAKES 4 SERVINGS

Corn and Crab Cakes

Fresh sweet corn and a dollop of Dijon mustard lend character to these tender, golden cakes. Enjoy them in this enticing salad presentation, as an appetizer, or serve them as sandwiches, slathering crisp rolls with the lively caper and mustard dressing.

6 cups mixed greens
½ cup sour cream (nonfat works fine)
1 tablespoon Dijon mustard
½ teaspoon drained capers
2 cups cooked crab, flaked
Kernels cut from 2 ears sweet corn
1 stalk celery, finely chopped
½ onion, finely chopped
¼ teaspoon kosher or sea salt
½ teaspoon freshly ground black pepper
2 tablespoons shredded fresh basil leaves
½ teaspoon chopped fresh lemon thyme leaves
2 eggs, lightly beaten
1 tablespoon olive oil
1 tablespoon butter

■ Divide the greens among 4 plates. In a small bowl, stir together the sour cream, mustard, and capers; set aside. In a mixing bowl, combine the crab, corn, celery, onion, salt, pepper, basil, thyme, and eggs. Form into 4 thin cakes.

■ In a frying pan, heat the olive oil and butter over medium-high heat and cook the cakes until golden brown, turning once, 3 to 4 minutes per side. Place a cake on each plate, drizzle with dressing, and serve.

Makes 4 servings

Fresh Tomato Pie

Use a range of ripe tomatoes to achieve the fullest possible flavor. Mix succulent heritage types like 'Brandywine', 'French Market', and 'Gardeners Delight' with new hybrids like 'Sweet Million', 'Sun Gold', and 'Oregon Sunrise'.

Pastry for one 8- to 9-inch pie crust
¼ teaspoon kosher or sea salt
¼ teaspoon freshly ground black pepper
2 cloves garlic, minced or pressed

2 tablespoons finely shredded fresh basil leaves
4 ripe tomatoes, cut in half and sliced
1 cup yellow cherry tomatoes, cut in half
1 cup red cherry tomatoes, cut in half
1 cup fine bread crumbs
½ cup coarsely grated fresh mozzarella
½ cup coarsely grated pecorino or Asiago cheese

■ Preheat the oven to 400°F. Line an 8- or 9-inch pie dish with the pastry, fluting the edges. Prick the crust all over with a fork and bake until lightly browned, 8 to 10 minutes. Leave the oven set at 400°F; set crust aside.

■ Blend together the salt, pepper, garlic, and basil, sprinkle over the cut tomatoes in a medium bowl, and let sit for 10 minutes. Gently layer the tomatoes into the pie shell with the bread crumbs and cheeses, beginning and ending with a light layer of bread crumbs and cheese. Bake until warmed through, 20 to 30 minutes. Serve at once.

Makes 6 servings

In the Northwest, small-fruited tomatoes fare better than large ones, which need more heat to ripen.

soups and stews

Cucumber and Avocado Soup

Even those who don't drink buttermilk enjoy the tartness it adds to this rich, smooth avocado and cucumber soup. When made thick, the jade-green soup is almost spreadable. For a thinner soup, add more buttermilk or some vegetable broth.

2 ripe avocados, diced
4 medium cucumbers, peeled and diced
½ teaspoon kosher salt
1 teaspoon fresh lemon thyme leaves
1 to 2 cups buttermilk
Flowers for garnish (pansy, viola,
      snapdragon, rose, or calendula)

■ Combine the avocados, cucumbers, salt, thyme, and 1 cup of the buttermilk in a blender or food processor. Pulse to chop, then blend or purée until the soup is the desired consistency. Add the remaining buttermilk if you prefer a thinner soup. Pour into shallow bowls, garnish with flowers, and serve.

MAKES 4 SERVINGS

'Sweet Success' cuke.

Cress and Fennel Soup

Florence or bulbing fennel takes on a velvety texture when marinated in oil, and its gentle sweetness delightfully balances peppery watercress. A touch of orange juice adds zip to this subtle soup. As always, when using citrus zest in a recipe, be sure to buy organic fruit to avoid eating pesticides and fungicides.

1 large or 2 small bulbs Florence fennel
    (about 8 ounces total), thinly sliced
2 stalks celery, thinly sliced
¼ to ½ cup olive oil
1 bunch watercress, stemmed
Juice and grated zest of 1 organic orange
3 cups chicken or vegetable broth
½ teaspoon salt
1 teaspoon freshly ground black pepper
¼ cup crumbled goat cheese, for garnish

■ Combine the sliced fennel and celery in a jar or storage container, add olive oil to cover, and marinate overnight, or for at least an hour. Drain, reserving the oil for salad dressing, and put the fennel and celery in a blender or food processor with the watercress, orange juice, orange zest, and 2 cups of the broth. Pulse to chop, then blend or purée until the soup is a chunky paste. Thin to the desired consistency with the remaining broth. Season with the salt and pepper. Pour the soup into shallow bowls, garnish with goat cheese, and serve.

Makes 4 servings

Summery Onion Soup

Onion lovers will lap up this uncooked version of the wintry classic soup. It is best made with mild Walla Walla Sweets but can also be made with Vidalia onions. Rounded yellow lemon cucumbers are excellent in this recipe.

4 Walla Walla Sweet onions, chopped
1 red Bermuda onion, finely chopped
2 to 3 cucumbers, peeled, seeded, and
    diced (4 cups)
½ teaspoon kosher salt
½ teaspoon ground black or white pepper
4 cups plain yogurt
4 garlic or chive blossoms, for garnish
4 teaspoons drained capers, for garnish

■ Combine the Walla Walla Sweets with half of the red onion, the cucumbers, salt, pepper, and yogurt in a blender or food processor. Pulse to chop, then blend or purée to the desired consistency. Stir in the remaining red onion. Pour into shallow bowls, garnish with chive blossoms and capers, and serve.

MAKES 4 SERVINGS

side dishes

Dilly Summer Vegetable Mixed Grill

For the deepest flavor, marinate the vegetables all day or overnight in a silky bath of olive oil and balsamic vinegar with fresh dill and thyme. However, save the tomatoes to add later, since chilling changes the sugars into starches, leaving these tender summer fruits tasting flat.

1 eggplant, cut into 1-inch-thick slices
4 small zucchini, sliced in half lengthwise
2 red bell peppers, cut into quarters
2 small yellow summer squash, cut in half lengthwise
2 tablespoons olive oil
1 tablespoon balsamic vinegar
1 clove garlic, minced or pressed
1 teaspoon fresh thyme leaves
1 teaspoon shredded fresh dill

¼ teaspoon salt
¼ teaspoon cracked black peppercorns
4 tomatoes, cut in half

■ Put all the vegetables except tomatoes into a large, resealable plastic bag. In a small jar, combine the remaining ingredients (olive oil through peppercorns), shake well to blend, and pour over the vegetables, squeezing gently through the bag to coat well. Marinate at least 1 hour or overnight in the refrigerator.

■ Start coals in a grill. A few minutes before you are ready to cook, remove vegetables from marinade and brush some of the marinade over the tomatoes. Grill the vegetables over medium-hot coals, 2 to 3 minutes per side. Serve at once.

MAKES 4 SERVINGS

cook's tip

Purée extra basil with olive oil (no garlic) and freeze in an ice-cube tray, then store in resealable freezer bags for up to 6 months. Add a cube to winter soups, sauces, and stews for a vivid reminder of summer.

Stuffed Cherry Tomatoes

For a lovely presentation and fabulous flavors, stuff a combination of 'Sun Gold' and 'Sweet Million' cherry tomatoes. The red and yellow fruits look very pretty together, and the contrast between tart-sweet 'Sun Golds' and juicy 'Sweet Millions' is delectable.

12 cherry tomatoes
½ cup crumbled goat cheese
½ cup minced fresh basil leaves
⅛ teaspoon salt
2 ounces pine nuts, toasted
½ teaspoon drained green peppercorns

■ Carefully core the cherry tomatoes, reserving the pulp. In a small bowl, combine the pulp with the goat cheese, basil, salt, pine nuts, and green peppercorns. Gently stuff the tomatoes with this mixture and serve.

MAKES 4 SERVINGS

Stir-Fried Asian Greens and Pea Vines

Nearly every market offers a decent selection of Asian greens, from bok choy and joi choy to tatsoi and mizuna. These range from tender to crisp and from peppery to sweet, so mix and match at will and revel in the variety. Tender pea vine tendrils (the growing tips) add delicate flavor and crunchy texture to any salad or side dish.

2 teaspoons vegetable oil
1 teaspoon sesame oil or peanut oil
1 small onion, thinly sliced
1- to 2-inch piece ginger root, peeled and
    chopped
1 cup thinly sliced bok choy
2 cups thinly sliced Asian greens (tatsoi,
    mizuna, joi choy, etc.)
1 cup thinly sliced young red kale
1 cup chopped pea vine tendrils
1 cup sugar or snap peas, trimmed
4 green onions, thinly sliced
1 tablespoon rice vinegar

1 tablespoon Thai sweet chili sauce or
   teriyaki sauce
1 tablespoon sesame seeds or chopped
   peanuts

■ Heat the oils in a wok over medium-high
heat. Add the remaining ingredients in the
order listed, stirring and cooking each for 30
seconds before adding the next. Serve at once.

MAKES 4 TO 6 SERVINGS

Margarita Sweet Corn

**Almost embarrassingly easy, this fat-free man-
ner of enjoying fresh sweet corn is simply and
utterly delicious. When you feed corn lovers,
double the recipe!**

4 ears sweet corn
1 lime, cut into quarters
Kosher or sea salt
Freshly ground black pepper

■ Start coals in a grill. Partially shuck corn,
leaving 1 or 2 layers of husk. Remove silk and
pull husks back up over ears. Grill the corn over
medium coals for 1 to 2 minutes per side. To
serve, shuck the corn and spritz it with fresh
lime juice, sprinkling with salt and pepper to
taste.

MAKES 4 SERVINGS

grilled Ancho, Sweet Onion, and Corn Salsa

This smoky, deeply flavorful concoction adds magic to grilled halibut or tuna as well as steak, turns a plain burger into manna, and gives the old chili dog new meaning. Make it ahead and chill for up to 4 days, or prepare it while your main dish grills. (Note: You can substitute jalapeño chiles for the anchos, if you like.)

1 tablespoon virgin olive oil
1 clove garlic, chopped
½ teaspoon fresh oregano leaves
2 or 3 ancho chiles, seeded and cut in half lengthwise
1 Walla Walla Sweet onion, thickly sliced
2 ears sweet corn, husked
Juice and grated zest of 1 organic orange
About ¼ teaspoon kosher or sea salt

■ Start coals in a grill or preheat the broiler. In a small bowl, combine the olive oil, garlic, and oregano. Brush or rub lightly over the chiles, onion, and corn. Grill or broil the vegetables until lightly blackened, 2 to 4 minutes per side, turning once. Wrap the chiles in a towel and set aside.

■ Coarsely chop the onion. Cut the corn kernels from the cobs. Rub the skin off the chiles and chop. In a serving bowl, combine the chiles, onions, and corn with the orange juice and zest, season with salt to taste, and serve.

MAKES ABOUT 2 CUPS

*Flowering borage (*Borago officinalis*).*

salads

Edible Flower Salad

This fluffy, flowery salad features a typical assortment of edible flowers that are blooming in my garden in June (violets, roses, calendula, and borage). Later in the summer, the peppery bite of nasturtium would add zip to this sweet mixture. Always use organically grown flowers only!

4 cups young greens
1 cup herb tips (fennel, dill, chives, cilantro, sage, lemon balm)
4 green onions, sliced
1 tablespoon fresh violets
1 tablespoon fresh calendula petals
1 tablespoon fresh borage flowers
1 tablespoon fresh rose petals

Dressing

2 tablespoons rice vinegar
⅓ cup virgin olive oil
1 teaspoon fresh lemon thyme leaves
¼ teaspoon kosher salt

■ Combine the greens, herb tips, and green onions in a large salad bowl, top with the flowers, and set aside.

■ To prepare the dressing, in a small jar, blend the vinegar, olive oil, lemon thyme, and salt. Drizzle over the salad, toss lightly, and serve at once.

MAKES 4 SERVINGS

cook's tip

flowers add appeal to savory and sweet recipes. Try tossing your next salad with Johnny-jump-ups or garnishing grilled fish with peppery nasturtiums. Drizzle steamed vegetables with fresh lime juice and a sprinkle of calendula petals. Serve chicken, shrimp, or jewel-toned fruit salads in colorful daylily cornucopias (remove the stamens first). On the sweet side, fill shortcakes with blueberries, raspberries, or strawberries and decorate them with clouds of whipped cream and a flutter of rose petals and pansies. For a party, make tiny shortcakes and top each tidbit with whipped cream and a fragrant rose petal.

Prawn Salad with Strawberries and Nectarines

Plump prawns, toasted walnuts, sweet fruit, and bitter greens provide alluring contrasts in this pretty main-dish summer salad.

3 tablespoons virgin olive oil
Juice and grated zest of 1 organic orange
1 tablespoon chopped fresh silver mint or spearmint
¼ teaspoon kosher salt
2 cups cooked, peeled prawns
2 cups young mixed greens
2 cups baby spinach, stemmed
1 cup shredded arugula and/or radicchio
½ small red onion, finely chopped
1 tablespoon shredded fresh lemon balm leaves
1 teaspoon fresh lemon thyme leaves
1 cup hulled, quartered strawberries
1 nectarine, thinly sliced
¼ cup chopped toasted walnuts

■ In a bowl or large jar, blend the olive oil, orange juice and zest, mint, and salt. Shake well, add the prawns, and set aside (this can be done ahead and chilled).

■ Combine all of the greens, the red onion, lemon balm, lemon thyme, strawberries, and nectarine in a large salad bowl. Remove prawns from dressing and add to the salad, then drizzle the dressing over the salad. Toss lightly, garnish with the walnuts, and serve at once.

MAKES 4 SERVINGS

Crisp Chicken Salad with Chipotle Cream Dressing

Toss crunchy bok choy with slivers of ruffled red cabbage, spicy arugula, sweet cherry tomatoes, and green onions. To wake up your senses, add fresh herbs with a generous hand, and top it off with Chipotle Cream Dressing, which also tastes fabulous on grilled chicken or fish.

2 cups shredded bok choy
1 cup finely shredded red cabbage

¼ cup shredded arugula

6 green onions, finely chopped

2 stalks celery, thinly sliced

1 tablespoon shredded fresh lemon balm leaves

½ teaspoon fresh thyme leaves

¼ cup fresh fennel tips, stemmed

¼ cup parsley leaves

½ cup 'Sun Gold' or any cherry tomatoes, halved

2 cups cooked chicken, cut into bite-sized pieces

2 tablespoons calendula or nasturtium petals, for garnish

Chipotle Cream Dressing

1 can (6 to 8 ounces) chipotle chiles in adobo sauce

1 cup crème fraîche, heavy cream, or sour cream (nonfat works fine)

1 clove garlic, minced

¼ teaspoon salt

¼ cup toasted sesame seeds

■ To prepare the Chipotle Cream Dressing, in a blender or food processor, purée the chiles with their sauce. Add 1 to 2 tablespoons (to taste) of the purée to the crème fraîche and stir well. Stir in the garlic, salt, and sesame seeds. Blend well. You will have about 1 cup. Store any unused chipotle purée in the refrigerator (in a squeeze bottle for easy use), where it keeps indefinitely.

■ In a large salad bowl, combine the bok choy, cabbage, arugula, green onions, celery, lemon balm, thyme, fennel, parsley, tomatoes, and chicken. Toss gently, drizzle with some of the dressing, and serve, garnished with flower petals. Save any remaining dressing for another use.

Makes 4 servings

Insalata di Fagioli e Tonno (Italian Tuna Salad)

This exotic-sounding salad is essentially an Italian tuna salad, glorified with ripe garden vegetables and fresh goat cheese. It is a scrumptious way to use leftover grilled tuna or salmon.

1½ cups fresh shelled beans, or 1 can (14 to 16 ounces) small white beans, rinsed and drained

6 cups young greens

¼ cup shredded fresh basil leaves

¼ cup shredded arugula leaves

12 cherry tomatoes, cut in half

1 small zucchini (about 4 inches long), thinly sliced

½ red onion, chopped

2 cups grilled tuna or salmon, flaked

⅓ cup virgin olive oil

¼ cup balsamic vinegar

1 clove garlic, minced

⅛ teaspoon kosher or sea salt

½ cup crumbled goat cheese or grated Asiago, for garnish

■ If using raw shell beans, steam until tender, about 10 minutes; set aside. In a large salad bowl, combine the greens, basil, arugula, cherry tomatoes, zucchini, red onion, and tuna. In a jar, combine the oil, vinegar, garlic, salt, and shell beans. Shake well to emulsify, strain out the beans, and add them to salad. Drizzle with the dressing, toss lightly, and serve, garnished with the cheese.

MAKES 4 ENTRÉE SERVINGS, 6 TO 8 SIDE DISH SERVINGS

cook's tip

fresh tomatoes should be used within a day or two of picking or purchase. Never store fresh tomatoes in the refrigerator, since cold temperatures will alter their chemical structure, changing sugars into starches and destroying much of the flavor.

Carrot-Marigold Salad

Spicy, lemon-scented signet marigolds provide a pleasing contrast to shredded sweet carrots. This is an intriguing and pretty side dish for grilled chicken or salmon.

1 cup finely shredded carrots
1 cup shredded bok choy
4 green onions, thinly sliced
1 tablespoon signet marigold petals

Dressing

¼ cup virgin olive oil
Juice and grated zest of 1 organic orange
½ teaspoon fresh tarragon leaves
¼ teaspoon kosher or sea salt
½ teaspoon drained capers
¼ teaspoon freshly ground black pepper

■ To prepare the dressing, in a jar, combine the olive oil, orange juice and zest, tarragon, salt, capers, and pepper. Shake well, and set aside.

■ Combine the carrots, bok choy, green onions, and marigold petals in a salad bowl, drizzle with the dressing, and toss gently. Serve at once.

MAKES 4 SERVINGS

Tomato and Nasturtium Salad with Basil Dressing

This beautiful, summery dish tastes as festive as it looks. Creamy mozzarella and the garlicky Basil Dressing perfectly offset the tart tomatoes and peppery nasturtiums. Always be sure that the flowers you eat are pesticide-free.

6 cups young mixed greens
2 to 3 ripe tomatoes, sliced
8 ounces fresh mozzarella, thinly sliced
⅛ teaspoon kosher salt
¼ cup nasturtium flowers, calyxes (leafy green bases) removed

Basil Dressing

¼ cup virgin olive oil
Juice and grated zest of 1 organic orange
2 cloves garlic, chopped
1 bunch fresh basil, stemmed and shredded
¼ cup walnuts, toasted
⅛ teaspoon kosher salt
1 teaspoon drained green peppercorns

■ To prepare the Basil Dressing, in a blender or food processor, combine the olive oil, orange juice and zest, garlic, basil, walnuts, and salt. Process until smooth, add the green peppercorns, and set aside.

■ Arrange the greens on 4 dinner plates, layer the sliced tomatoes and mozzarella on top, and scatter with the remaining salt. Drizzle the dressing over the salads, garnish with the nasturtiums, and serve at once.

MAKES 4 SERVINGS

Fresh Corn Salad with Sweet Chili–Lime Dressing

The clean, singing flavors all come through here, from the tender sweet corn to the heat of the chili sauce. Those who can't take raw corn can microwave the corn for 1 minute before tossing it into the salad. The flavors intensify if this salad is made ahead and chilled.

2 cups sweet corn kernels (cut from about 4 ears)

1 red onion, chopped
1 bunch cilantro, stemmed
1 cup shredded bok choy
1 cup shredded red cabbage
¼ cup roasted peanuts

Sweet Chili–Lime Dressing

Juice and grated zest of 1 organic lime
1 clove garlic, chopped
¼ cup Thai sweet red chili sauce

■ To prepare the Sweet Chili-Lime Dressing, in a jar, combine the lime juice and zest, garlic, and Thai chili sauce. Shake well; set aside.

■ In a serving bowl, combine the corn, onion, cilantro, bok choy, and cabbage. Drizzle with the dressing and toss gently to coat. Chill or serve at once, garnished with the peanuts.

MAKES 4 TO 6 SERVINGS

Red, White, and Blueberry Salad with Fireworks Dressing

Bursting with fruit, sharp cheddar cheese, Walla Walla Sweets, and pop-in-your-mouth tomatoes, this summery salad goes well with anything you care to grill. Serve it with Fireworks Dressing for a delightfully explosive experience. If you are feeding "heat weenies," use less-exuberant quantities of the chipotles or the green curry sauce in the dressing.

4 cups young salad greens

1 bunch red arugula, stemmed

1 cup flat Italian parsley leaves

1 cup shredded fresh basil leaves

1 Walla Walla Sweet onion, finely diced

1 cup finely diced extra-sharp white
   cheddar cheese

1 pint blueberries, stemmed

1 pint grape or cherry tomatoes, stemmed

Fireworks Dressing

½ cup virgin olive oil

¼ to ⅓ cup cider vinegar or wine vinegar

2 cloves garlic, minced

1 to 2 teaspoons puréed chipotle chiles in
   adobo sauce or Thai green curry sauce

■ To prepare the Fireworks Dressing, combine the olive oil, vinegar, and garlic in a covered jar and shake well to blend. Add the puréed chipotles to taste, starting with 1 teaspoon. You will have about 1 cup dressing.

■ In a salad bowl, toss the greens and herbs gently. Top with the onion, cheese, blueberries, and tomatoes. Pass with the dressing. Save any remaining dressing for another use.

MAKES 8 SERVINGS

cook's tip

here in the maritime Northwest, parsley can be harvested year-round. Flat Italian parsley has the most complex and subtle flavor, so cook with that one and save the pretty, frilly kinds for garnishes.

Summer Coleslaw with Fresh Tomatillo Salsa

Fresh tomatillos have a delicate, tart flavor that makes a memorable sauce for fish, chicken, or grilled vegetables. Try the zippy tomatillo salsa over anything from burgers to brown rice, or use it as a fat-free dressing for salad greens, steamed vegetables, or warm potato salad.

2 cups shredded red cabbage

2 cups shredded green cabbage

2 cups shredded Chinese cabbage or bok choy

1 sweet carrot, shredded

1 unpeeled dessert apple, such as Braeburn, cored and shredded

Fresh Tomatillo Salsa

1 to 2 serrano chiles

1 red bell pepper

2 cups ripe tomatillos, husked and cut in half

1 Walla Walla Sweet onion, chopped

1 bunch cilantro, stemmed

¼ teaspoon kosher or sea salt

½ cup rice vinegar

■ To prepare the Fresh Tomatillo Salsa, in a dry frying pan over medium-high heat, roast the serrano chiles and red bell pepper until blackened on all sides. Wrap in a towel and let cool. Rub off the skin, and seed and chop the peppers. Combine with the tomatillos, onion, cilantro, salt, and vinegar in a blender or food processor. Purée to a coarse slurry.

■ Combine the cabbages, carrot, and apple in a salad bowl and toss with the salsa dressing. Serve at room temperature or chilled.

MAKES 4 TO 6 SERVINGS

Carrots with Raspberry Purée

When your summer garden yields sweet, crunchy carrots, or when you find them in the market, toss them in a satiny raspberry purée for an unforgettable "wow" moment.

　　2 cups peeled, grated sweet carrots
　　¼ teaspoon kosher or sea salt
　　1 teaspoon fructose or honey (optional)
　　1 cup fresh raspberries, puréed

■ In a serving bowl, combine the carrots and salt; set aside. Stir the fructose or honey, if using, into the raspberry purée and let sit for 10 minutes. Toss the carrots with the purée and serve at once.

MAKES 4 SERVINGS

Harvesting 'Nelson' carrots.

baked goods and sweets

Cherries with Fresh Fruit Dipping Sauce

One of my favorite picnic treats is a huge bowl of cherries over ice with a tangy, soupy dipping sauce. There is something magical about the tart-sweet slitheriness of chilled cherries on a hot day at the beach. This recipe is equally delicious as an appetizer or as a dessert with very good vanilla ice cream.

4 to 5 pounds cherries with stems
1 bag chipped ice
Juice and grated zest of 1 organic orange
Juice and grated zest of 1 organic lime
1 cup raspberries
1 cup strawberries
1 unpeeled sweet red apple, cored and
    diced
1 to 2 tablespoons fructose or brown sugar
    (optional)

■ Wash the cherries, and arrange them in a deep bowl. Put the ice in a larger bowl and set the cherry bowl over the ice. In a blender or food processor, combine the orange juice and zest, lime juice and zest, raspberries, strawberries, and apple. Purée to a slush and add fructose or brown sugar to taste, if desired. Cover the sauce and chill until serving time.

MAKES 4 TO 8 SERVINGS

Lemon Sorbet with Huckleberry Sauce

This voluptuous taste treat makes a lovely party dessert. Fructose boosts natural fruit flavors without excessive sugariness, but sugar works fine too.

1 pint huckleberries, stemmed
½ cup rather sweet white wine (such as gewürztraminer)
1 to 3 tablespoons fructose or sugar
2 pints white lemon sorbet (or any high-quality lemon sorbet)
Mint leaves, for garnish

■ In a blender or food processor, combine the huckleberries, wine, and fructose or sugar to taste (start with 1 tablespoon), and purée.

■ Scoop the sorbet into serving dishes, and pour sauce over the sorbet. Garnish with mint leaves and serve.

Makes 6 to 8 servings

fructose versus sugar

When I cooked a lot for a diabetic friend, I learned to use fructose, a natural fruit sugar, to enhance the flavor of all fruits and vegetables. You can use as little as a quarter to a third as much fructose as you would table sugar in recipes involving fruits, from sorbets to tarts and cobblers.

A tiny pinch of fructose blooms the natural sweetness in steamed carrots and asparagus and awakens unsuspected depths in parsnips and turnips. If a tomato-based pasta sauce seems flat, a tad of fructose will pick it up remarkably. I use fructose to enhance not-quite-ripe strawberries, to give pumpkin or squash dishes a luscious finish, and to make no-longer-youthful peas taste fresher.

Fructose isn't a good choice for sweetening ordinary baked goods like brownies, but it will make outstanding pumpkin pie and flavorful freezer jam, and will even give lemonade a lift. In fruity dishes like rhubarb and apple pie, adjust the amount to suit your own taste, but you'll find you can consistently get a better flavor with just a little fructose.

Raspberry-Blueberry Rollups

Thai spring roll skins or wrappers are soft, chewy, tapioca-based wraps that are fat free, very low in calories, and wheat free to boot. Dip each brittle circle in a bowl of hot tap water to soften it a bit, then roll it up around almost anything, from salad to stir-fry. They may look lumpy and uneven at first, but within half an hour, the translucent wraps even out, showcasing fresh fruit, crème fraîche, and orange zest.

Juice and grated zest of 1 organic orange
1 tablespoon sugar
1 cup fresh blueberries
1 cup fresh raspberries
1 cup crème fraîche or sour cream (nonfat works fine)
8 Thai spring roll skins or wrappers

■ Rub 1 teaspoon of the orange zest into the sugar, mashing to release the citrus oils.

■ Gently toss the berries with the orange juice and set aside. Blend remaining zest into the crème fraîche. Gently fold together the sugar and cream mixtures.

■ Dip a spring roll skin into warm water to soften, place on a plate, and place about ¼ cup fruit on the upper third of the wrap. Fold the top 2 to 3 inches of the wrap down over the filling, fold in both sides, and roll up. Repeat with the remaining filling and skins. Let stand until opaque, about 20 minutes.

■ Arrange 2 rollups on each of 4 plates and serve, garnished with the crème fraîche.

MAKES 4 SERVINGS

Italian Baked Peaches with Peach Whipped Cream

When you need an elegant dessert, this fragrant beauty fits the bill. It's also terrific made with nectarines.

4 large, ripe peaches
⅓ cup butter, at room temperature
⅓ cup brown sugar
¾ cup ground or finely chopped almonds
2 tablespoons amaretto or marsala

Peach Whipped Cream

1 cup heavy cream
¼ teaspoon almond or vanilla extract
1 to 2 teaspoons sugar
½ cup mashed or puréed ripe peach

■ To prepare the Peach Whipped Cream, beat the cream to the desired consistency. Fold in the almond extract and sugar to taste, starting with 1 teaspoon. Fold in the peach purée and chill until serving time. Refrigerate any leftovers.

■ Preheat the oven to 350°F. Bring a medium saucepan of water to a boil. With a deep ladle, dip the peaches in the boiling water for 2 or 3 seconds. Remove from the water and slip off the skins. Cut in half and remove the pits, scraping away any red veins. Place the peaches, cut side up, in a baking dish. Mash the butter and brown sugar together, then blend in the ground almonds.

■ Fill the peach centers with the almond mixture and bake for 20 minutes. Add some amaretto to each peach and bake until bubbly, another 10 to 15 minutes. Serve warm or cold, topped with the whipped cream.

MAKES 4 TO 8 SERVINGS

cook's tip

For flavorful peaches, choose firm but tender-feeling fruit without soft spots. The heaviest peaches are the most juicy, and fully ripe fruit has a faint, fruity scent that tells you it's ripe. Use ripe peaches within a day or two of picking or purchase, and never store them in the refrigerator, which will ruin the fresh, full flavor.

Huckleberry-Hazelnut Upside-Down Cake

Make this simple crowd-pleaser with almost any summery fruit—Italian prune plums, nectarines, peaches, raspberries, or loganberries. As the kids say, it's all good!

⅓ cup plus 1 tablespoon butter, softened
1 cup firmly packed brown sugar
1 cup toasted, skinned, chopped hazelnuts
2 cups huckleberries, stemmed
½ cup whole wheat pastry flour
½ cup pastry flour or unbleached white
  flour
1 teaspoon baking powder
¼ teaspoon ground coriander
¼ teaspoon salt
4 eggs, separated
1 teaspoon vanilla extract
1 cup sugar, sifted

■ Preheat the oven to 400°F. In a heavy, 10-inch cast-iron skillet, melt ⅓ cup butter over medium heat. Add the brown sugar and cook, stirring, until bubbly, 2 to 3 minutes. Add the hazelnuts and cook, stirring, for 2 minutes. Remove from heat and line the bottom of the pan with the huckleberries.

■ In a medium bowl, sift together the flours, baking powder, coriander, and salt. In a small bowl, gently beat the egg yolks, blending in the remaining 1 tablespoon butter and the vanilla. Whip the egg whites until stiff but not dry, adding the sugar, 1 tablespoon at a time. Fold in the egg yolks, then gently stir in the flour mixture, ⅓ cup at a time. Turn the oven down to 350°F, spoon the batter over the huckleberries, and bake until golden, 20 to 30 minutes.

■ Let cool in the skillet for 5 minutes, then invert the cake onto a plate and serve with the fruit-side up.

MAKES 4 TO 6 SERVINGS

Summer Garden Shake

This is just an example of how delicious fresh shakes made with whatever the garden offers can be. In season, you might use nectarines, marionberries, huckleberries, or peaches instead of raspberries and strawberries.

> 2 cups vanilla soymilk, or 2 cups milk and ½ teaspoon vanilla extract
> 1 cup raspberries
> 1 cup strawberries, cut in half
> 1 teaspoon shredded fresh lemon balm leaves
> 1 teaspoon shredded fresh fruit sage leaves
> 1 teaspoon shredded fresh mint leaves
> 1 tablespoon honey or brown sugar
> ¼ teaspoon ground nutmeg

■ Combine all ingredients in a blender and purée to the desired consistency. Serve at once.

Makes 2 servings

cook's tip

fresh and fragrant, lemon balm has a crisp, clean flavor that lends itself well to everything from spicy salads to sweet desserts. A number of ornamental forms are available with golden, chartreuse, or cream-variegated foliage. All taste the same, with a brisk, lemony tang. Chop the fresh foliage and add it to soups, salads, sautés, and stir-fries, or to iced teas and lemonades. Add dried leaves to bath salts, sachets, and potpourri, or mix a few with green tea and rose petals to make a refreshing drink.

summer gardening calendar

what to plant	Basil, beans, celery, cilantro, corn, cucumbers, eggplant, leeks, lettuce, melons, parsley, parsnips, peppers, potatoes, pumpkins, squash, tomatoes, tomatillos, watermelon, zucchini
what to harvest	Basil, beans, berries, carrots, celery, cilantro, corn, cucumbers, edible flowers, eggplant, lavender, leeks, lemon balm, lettuce, melons, okra, parsley, parsnips, peaches, peppers, potatoes, pumpkins, squash, tomatoes, tomatillos, melons, zucchini
what's in the market	Basil, beans, berries, celery, cherries, cilantro, corn, cucumbers, eggplant, leeks, lettuce, melons, okra, parsley, parsnips, peaches, peppers, potatoes, pumpkins, squash, tomatoes, tomatillos, melons, zucchini

gardening notes for summer ingredients

■ *Basil* Start basil in spring, keeping the plants indoors until warm weather arrives. Cool nights are devastating to tropicals, so wait until soil temperatures are consistently in the high 50s before setting out basil and other heat lovers. Young basil plants will be a lot bushier if you pinch out the first stem tips above the third set of true leaves. Basil prefers compost over fertilizer and needs moderate but consistent amounts of water to produce bountiful crops.

Fragrant basil.

Large-leaf basil like 'Genovese' or 'Mammoth Sweet' makes wonderful leafy wraps for grilled prawns or vegetable strips. Shred lemon basil over grilled fish or steamed vegetables, and decorate soups or salads with tasty leaves of 'Purple Ruffles'.

Harvest the growing tips to promote bushiness and keep the plant from blooming (which decreases foliage production).

■ *Beans* Both string beans and shelling beans are tropical crops that need warm soil (over 60°F) to perform well. Sow after Memorial Day in mounded beds in full sun. Amend the soil well with compost and feed with a complete organic fertilizer. Provide trellis panels or netting for pole beans to scramble up, or grow compact bush beans without extra support.

Beans need only moderate feeding (every few weeks), but they do require even moisture to crop properly. Keep the foliage dry to avoid diseases, and mulch well with compost to maintain soil moisture. New varieties are richer in flavor and more disease resistant than some old standbys. I still swear by 'Kentucky Wonder' pole beans, but I also appreciate the succulent 'Nugget' for yellow string beans. For bush beans, I like the

jumbo but tender 'Jade'. Skinny little filet beans are best harvested when young and tender, and I find that 'Nickel' holds up really well in our region. The mottled rose-and-cream 'Dragon Tongue' beans can be eaten as snap beans; left to ripen, they can be harvested as fresh beans for shelling or gathered late as dried beans (terrific for soups).

*Bush beans (*Phaseolus vulgaris *'Vermont Cranberry').*

■ *Blackberries, Dewberries, Boysenberries, Loganberries, Marionberries, and Tayberries* The relentless spread of rampant weedy blackberries tells us clearly that blackberries love the Northwest. Our own native dewberry, a ground-hugging trailer, has an exquisite flavor unmatched by

Strawberry 'Seascape', red raspberry 'Tulameen', blueberry 'Duke', golden raspberries, marionberries, and boysenberries.

anything in commerce. However, male dewberry plants are more common than females, so you may need to root cuttings of fruitful plants and transplant them into your own yard to get great fruit set.

The region boasts a number of special varieties that are best grown here, all of which have similar cultivation requirements. Give blackberries plenty of room in a sunny spot, and plant them in mounded beds or in any well-drained soil amended with grit or crushed sand and ample compost.

Blackberries fruit on old wood, so each season's fresh canes will be next year's fruit bearers. Since there are several types of blackberries, each needing a specific type of staking and pruning—for which timing is critical—consult a good garden manual like Sunset's *Western Garden Book* to guide you.

■ *Blueberries* Beautiful, bushy blueberries are East Coast cousins to our native huckleberries and grow just as happily in Northwestern gardens. Like huckleberries, blueberries prefer woodsy, humus-rich soils that offer a deep, cool root run. Unlike huckleberries, they grow best in full sun; plant in fall or early spring to fully establish. If your yard has a boggy area, plant them on a mound just above the soggy soil. Choose from early, midseason, or late croppers, or plant all three to enjoy plump, tart blueberries all summer. Where huckleberries are already growing, your blueberries probably won't need a pollinator partner, but choose several kinds of each type anyway, for the sake of variety.

Moisture-loving blueberries appreciate heavy, acid soils as long as they are well amended with generous amounts of compost. A deep (3- to 4-inch) compost mulch around blueberry plants will help keep down weeds while conserving moisture and feeding the soil biota that help plant roots dine well.

Sawdust is often used for blueberry mulch, but be sure always to use old, well-rotted sawdust or your plants may suffer from nitrogen deficiency (all wood products pull nitrogen from the soil as they rot). More complex in nutrients, mature compost is a better choice in the long run.

Blueberries rarely require pruning, but you can lightly thin the twiggy, berry-bearing branches of mature blueberries if you prefer to harvest fewer but larger fruits. Fruit cages or bird netting will help you beat the birds to the berries.

■ *Carrots* Like all root crops, carrots grow best in deep, well drained soil that is rich in compost and free of rocks, roots, and other obstacles to growth. Sow short rows of carrots in a sunny spot every few weeks from late March through mid to late July. Cover early sowings with lightweight row cover fabric to avoid carrot fly maggots.

For crisp, flavorful summer carrots, try 'Rodelika', 'Healthmaster' (packed with extra vitamins), tender 'Mokum', and crunchy 'Napa'. If your last sowing is of winter-hardy carrots, you may want to sow several larger rows to harvest through fall and winter. 'Autumn King', 'Nelson', 'Bolero', and 'Merida' are great winter keepers, as is the extremely tasty 'Nantaise'.

Organic carrots.

■ *Cucumbers* These heat-lovers are fusspots in maritime gardens, where they need preferential treatment to perform well. Give them a sunny spot in well-drained soil that's generously enriched with compost, and mulch each plant deeply with compost after the soil is well warmed up (mid to high 60s). Special mulches of silvery, reflective material help boost yields, and floating row covers like Reemay help create a beneficial microclimate that's pet free and even in temperature.

Start seed indoors in late spring in plantable pots to avoid root disturbance, and give each plant at least 3 feet of elbow room; plant out in summer, or after the last frost date. Feed weekly with a complete organic fertilizer (like a 5-5-5), and water consistently until the cukes are well filled out. Chose disease-resistant varieties like Green Slam and Poinsett 97 for best cropping.

■ *Edible Flowers* Summer celebrations of all kinds are made more festive with flowery edible garnishes. Before you experiment, take time to research a bit to be sure the flowers are nontoxic, and always be sure that the flowers you eat are pesticide free (systemic pesticides are toxic to people as well as to plant pests). Nontoxic

Salad with basil, Tyee spinach, dill, chives, and pea blossoms.

flowers include organically grown roses, violets, pansies, calendulas, nasturtiums, snapdragons, daylilies, and edible culinary herb blossoms such as chamomile, basil, rosemary, and mint. Other good garnish flowers include puffy purple garlic and chive blossoms, whose little explosions of color make the simplest soup look fancy.

Wonder which flowers can safely be used at weddings and other festive events? You'll find a website with lots of information about edible flowers at *www.ext.colostate.edu/pubs/garden/07237.html*.

The author, Steve Newman, wrote to me: "One thing that you need to remind people about is that allergic responses are unpredictable. Also, there are many who like to preserve flowers for cakes using recipes from our 'favorite' culinary/gardening/style specialists using egg whites. People need to use the pasteurized egg white mixes from the dairy section to avoid any potential food poisoning risks."

■ *Garden Greens* These easily grown leafy greens are alike in preferring a sunny spot in well-drained soil with compost and a bit of alfalfa meal rather than fertilizer as such. All need moderate moisture during their active growth periods, and most self-sow if allowed to go to seed.

Arugula or Rocket The rough, slightly bitter quality of arugula makes it a favorite in European spring tonics and dishes of early greens. A member of the mustard clan, it gets tough with old age. Sow short rows of arugula in winter (under cover) through spring and again in late summer for fall picking.

Bok Choy Sow short rows in late winter (under cover) and early spring and again in late summer for fall and winter harvest. Afternoon shade and deep mulches to conserve moisture help keep bok choy from bolting in summer heat.

Chinese Cabbage Sow short rows in early summer to midsummer, protecting plants with woven row cover (like Reemay) to avoid cabbage moths and maggots. Afternoon shade and deep mulches help keep these slow headers from bolting in summer heat. To extend the harvest, add cloches or row cloth tunnels as winter closes in.

Corn Salad Tender and delicately flavored, this lowly weed (known in Europe as mâche) is delightful in salads or cooked with other greens, and it can be cropped pretty much year round in the Northwest. Sow corn salad in summer for

Prolific organic greens.

fall and winter crops and in late winter (under cover) through spring for spring and summer picking. All it needs to thrive is compost and a light sprinkling of alfalfa meal in early spring and midfall. Give corn salad a patch of its own and let it go to seed in midsummer. You'll find your fall crop waiting for you for free!

Cress Watercress grows best along a flowing stream but can be quite happy in mounded beds amended with grit or crushed sand and lots of compost. It needs deep mulch to conserve moisture, and regular watering. American or winter cress grows happily in beds and borders, flourishing year-round without any particular care. European salad cress can be grown in the kitchen, in little flats (the kind you can buy wheat grass growing in) or in bowls with drain holes. Sow a fresh panful every few weeks and harvest as you like.

Endive and Escarole Curly or frilly endive and plainer escarole are both chicory cousins with tender, crisp foliage used in salads, sautés, and stir-fries. Sow in mid to late summer for fall through winter cropping (under cover, by that time).

Radicchio This popular Italian salad green, pronounced rah-DEE-key-oh, has become an American favorite as well in recent years. Red-leafed radicchio is a chicory cousin that can be sown in short rows from late winter (under cover) into spring and again in summer for fall cropping.

Shiso (Leaf Mustard) Sow shiso in short rows from late winter (under cover) through mid-spring and again in late summer or early fall. A quick cropper, it is also handsome enough for a place in the border. Red or green, large leaf or small, shiso has a pleasantly piquant flavor.

■ *Lavender* Hardy, evergreen lavender grows best in well-drained soil in full sun. Give lavender compost rather than fertilizer, though a moderate transplant fertilizer like Whitney Farms' Smart Start is a good idea, since it feeds the soil as well as the plant. When lavender is grown lean, with little or no summer water and no fertilizer, it offers the most concentrated essential oils, the best flavor, and the fullest fragrance.

Lavender flowers are usually used dry, though fresh florets may be tossed into soups and salads as well as lemonade and shortbread cookies. To harvest lavender, pick the flower stems before the florets are fully open along the entire stalk. Place them on a drying rack or a clean window

Lavender angustifolia *'Hidcote'*.

screen in a cool, dry place away from direct sunlight, shaking them gently every day or so to be sure they dry evenly. To store, pull the dry florets off the stems and keep them in a clean jar with a tightly fitting lid. Store in a dark cupboard for up to 3 months or in the freezer (double-wrap for freshness) for up to 6 months.

■ *Lemon Balm* Bushy, almost shrubby lemon balm is among the easiest herbs to grow in the Northwest. Plant spring or fall, and for fullest flavor, grow lemon balm in full sun, adding compost rather than fertilizer and watering only when a plant looks slightly wilted. Mature plants may never need watering, but they may need trimming to keep them in bounds. One plant is probably enough for most kitchens, as this enduring, hardy herb is an enthusiastic self-sower and very persistent in gardens. Harvest the largest leaves fresh for best flavor. In mild years, lemon balm may be used year-round, but even after a cold winter, it is always ready for use by March or April.

*Variegated lemon balm (*Melissa officinalis *'Variegata').*

■ *Peaches* Years ago, I wanted to grow my own peaches. I bought a Frost peach tree (resistant to leaf curl) and waited. And waited. After five years, my little tree finally birthed three peaches. They tasted all right, but nothing like the sun-ripened peaches from Yakima. Peaches really do like heat, and warm nights are something maritime gardeners just can't supply.

If you really want your own peaches, place your tree 5 to 10 feet away from a south-facing wall, which will reflect more heat and light to the fruit. (Fall is the best time to plant.) Prune the tree to a low framework (look for a low-grafted tree to simplify this task) and study a pruning guide to learn what fruiting spurs look like (fat and squat) so you don't chop them off in misplaced pruning zeal.

Mulch peach trees with compost each spring and fall to enhance the flavor, and thin the crop to one fruit per spur to improve the size of the fruit.

■ *Raspberries* Raspberries flourish in sunny gardens, either in mounded beds amended with grit or crushed sand and compost, or in well-drained soil, again compost-amended. In both cases, raspberry canes should be generously mulched with compost to suppress weeds and feed the soil. (Compost helps produce sweeter fruit.)

There are many kinds of raspberries to grow, with red, yellow, black, or purple fruit that crops early, midseason, or late. Dozens of named forms are available, and like blackberries, each type of plant has specific training and pruning requirements. Again, you are best off consulting a good garden manual like Sunset's *Western Garden Book* to guide you through the necessary seasonal chores.

■ *Sweet Corn* Sweet or sugar corn needs to be grown well away from popcorn or feed corn to avoid producing ears with tough, mealy kernels. Corn is a heat-loving crop that can't be set outside until the soil is warm (in the mid to high 60s). Start it from seed indoors in late spring or early summer in paper pots, then plant the seedlings pot and all to avoid root disturbance. Corn is wind-pollinated and needs company to produce well. In small gardens, plant it in 6- by 6-foot blocks in staggered rows, placing the plants 18 to 24 inches apart. Give these heavy feeders plenty of organic fertilizer and keep them evenly moist until the ears are fully filled out.

Green globe artichoke, super sweet 'Jubilee' corn, zucchini, zinnias, and salvia flowers.

■ *Sweet Onions* Walla Walla Sweets can be grown from seed in summer and enjoyed as green onions in fall, then harvested over the winter as full-sized onions. Vidalias and mild red onions like Bermudas are usually planted in spring for summer and fall harvest. Like all root crops, onions need deep, well-drained soil and can be grown best in mounded beds amended with grit or crushed sand and compost. Plant sets as soon as you find them in nurseries (usually in February), and start harvesting when the young onions are 2 inches across.

■ *Tomatillos* Like their cousins the Chinese lantern perennials, annual tomatillos carry their fruit tucked inside papery husks that resemble little vellum lampshades. As the fruit ripens, the husks split open and the cherry-sized fruit tumbles to the ground. Start from seed indoors, moving plants outside when the soil is warm (in the 60s). These tart, tangy fruits need a fellow pollinator, so plant in clusters of three to five, setting plants about 2 feet apart, for best fruit set.

Tomatillos are very easy to grow, but unlike their Chinese lantern cousins, they won't take over the garden. Most tomatillos have a sweet-tart flavor with earthy overtones, but a few (like

*Purple tomatillo (*Physalis ixocarpa*).*

'Aunt Molly's') are quite sweet and can be made into jams and sweet tart fillings. Most often, tomatillos are used in fresh salsas or in spicy chile verde sauces.

■ *Tomatoes* Tender tropicals, tomatoes can be grown year-round (and for years at a stretch) if you bring them into a heated greenhouse as summer wanes. Usually, though, we treat them as annuals and enjoy their bounty from midsummer into fall.

In the maritime Northwest, small-fruited tomatoes like 'Sun Gold' and 'Sweet Million' do better than the hunky 'Big Boy', which needs a lot of heat to ripen properly. Extra-early varieties like 'Oregon Spring', 'Early Cascade', and 'Matina' set fruit well even in cool years.

Start tomatoes from seed in late winter, or buy husky plants to set out when all frosts are past (usually around Memorial Day in maritime regions). Feed them every week with mild fertilizer (like a 5-5-5), and use a transplant fertilizer like Whitney Farms' Smart Start, which contains beneficial biota, when you plant them into the garden.

Use plenty of compost when you plant, and mulch deeply (3 to 4 inches) with compost as well, giving each plant at least a 2- to 3-foot circle of compost. For stronger plants, bury several inches of tomato stem when you set out your plants.

Tomatoes need consistent water to ripen well, but they can develop numerous foliage diseases unless you are careful to water only the roots. A new transplant should be watered sparingly, but a well-rooted young plant may need a gallon of water a day, and a big one that's heavy with fruit may need 5 gallons two to three times a week.

Yellow beans, cherry tomatoes, and heliotrope.

fall | *september october november*

September is Organic Food

Celebration Month. That makes the start of fall a great time to salute the hard-working farmers and commercial organic food growers who are willing to put out the extra energy, thought, and attention it takes to grow whole-some, healthy food without poisons. It's also a good time to cheer on home gardeners who are raising backyard food crops the organic way.

Start an organic vegetable garden

If you haven't yet grown your own food organically, fall is a terrific time to give it a try. It is actually a very simple process. Here in the maritime Northwest, organic vegetable gardening is especially easy, since we are blessed with a mild climate that offers us an extremely long season for growing a huge range of edibles.

To get started, lay out your beds running north and south. For ease of harvest, keep the beds about 4 feet wide and as long as you want them. This way, anything you plant can readily be reached from either side of the bed. Divide your beds with paths that are at least 2 to 3 feet wide so you can get a loaded cart or wheelbarrow along them when your plants are lush and full-grown.

The ideal bed is made with clean topsoil and compost that's mounded at least 12 inches above the original soil level. Slope the sides gently for about 8 inches on each side, leaving a broad, flat top surface about 40 inches wide for planting. Top-dress the beds with 2 to 3 inches of mature compost or composted dairy manure. When growing food crops, it is wise to use organically certified compost as well as topsoil. Organic certification ensures that the compost and topsoil are free of pathogens like *E. coli*, and don't contain problematic amounts of pesticides or other pollutants.

Mounded beds do not need to be made in boxes, and most definitely not boxes built of pressure-treated lumber, which releases measurable amounts of toxins into damp soil. Instead, simply mulch with compost to prevent erosion. Better yet, plant those sloping sides with hardy herbs and simple flowers to attract bees and other pollinators to your garden.

Overleaf: Sunflowers and fall gourds. Right: Raised beds of vegetables, flowers, and herbs amid a garden house retreat.

Yes, this means you can't till. Today, we know that tilling is not a beneficial practice for healthy soil. Instead of chewing up the soil layers, simply layer on amendments each season, from soy and cottonseed meals to dolomite lime, kelp, rock dust, and compost. Layering is a benign way to enrich the soil without unduly disturbing soil biotic colonies.

Mulch the paths between the beds 4 to 6 inches deep with shredded bark, straw, or any organic material you like, from sawdust or wood shavings to hazelnut shells. Do not use grass for paths, as it will constantly invade your beds, making extra work and robbing nutrients from your crops.

Beds made in fall can be planted with late-season crops like onions, garlic, and leeks as well as kale, chard, and winter cabbages. If you leave them until spring, the top-dressing of compost or composted dairy manure will keep them clean and free of weeds until you are ready to plant.

Replenish nutrients in the established garden

For those with established gardens, fall is the time to harvest, restore soil quality, and prepare beds for the slow winter season. Harvesting crops is what gardening is all about, yet each time we remove nutrients in the form of plant material like cabbages and corn, we deplete the soil. In sustainable agriculture, the goal is to close the nutrient loop as much as possible, keeping plant material in place by returning what we remove in the form of compost. Since what we eat is not returned (for numerous good reasons), we need to add nutrients. This is done by annual mulching with compost and by the addition of simple organic fertilizers such as Whitney Farms, Organica, and similar products.

We can also restore soil nutrient levels by sowing cover crops. Winter wheat or rye, field peas, annual clovers, buckwheat, and alfalfa are common cover crops that are sown in late summer or fall and then chopped up in late winter or early spring. The top growth and the roots both degrade quickly, leaving the soil replenished and ready to plant.

As autumn sets the leaves on fire, it awakens in us a desire for delicious, warm food, flickering fires, and deep comfort. The recipes in this section will help you ease into the busy, bustling holidays. In the following pages, you'll find plenty of simple, beautiful, and tasty dishes that will help you spend your time enjoying your family and guests instead of slaving alone in the kitchen. Remember that cooking together is far more fun, and kitchen time can be very convivial when guests are invited to participate.

Autumn oils and vinegars

This fall, when local markets are overflowing with fabulous locally grown vegetables and fruit, take advantage of the bounty by making tasty meals based on these splendid fresh ingredients. One really simple way to start is by making your own herbal oils and vinegars, storing up the last gasp of summer to brighten the darkness of winter yet to come.

To make instant herbal oils that can be used fresh for 2 to 3 weeks, use a variation of this simple recipe, exchanging basil for cilantro, thyme, or the herb of your choice.

Basil Oil

By summer's end, basil is often as big as a bushel basket. Use it fresh in savory herb butters like the one on page 185, or blend any extra with a little olive oil and freeze for use in winter dressings, soups, and stews.

2 cups fresh basil leaves
2 cups virgin olive oil

■ Roll the basil lightly with a rolling pin, and pack it into a clean jar. Cover with the oil, seal the jar, and place in a cool, dark cupboard for 2 weeks. Shake the jar lightly every day or so. Check the strength after 2 weeks. When the oil is infused to your taste, strain it into a clean jar, seal tightly, and refrigerate for up to 3 months.

MAKES ABOUT 2 CUPS

To make longer-lasting oil, pack a clean jar with the herb (such as basil), then cover with virgin olive oil or canola oil. Let the oil stand in a cool, dim place (like a kitchen cupboard) for 1 to 2 weeks. Shake the jar gently each day and taste the oil frequently to see how the flavor is coming along. When the oil tastes the way you like it, strain out the herbs and decant the oil into a new, clean jar. Store in a cool, dry place out of direct light, as you would any cooking oil.

You can also do the same thing with peeled garlic cloves, shallots, chile peppers, or rose petals (be sure the roses were organically grown and not treated with systemic rose pesticides). If you use garlic or shallots, remove them from the oil once they have flavored it, or the oil will become too strongly flavored in time to be pleasant. To make citrus-flavored oils, peel thin slices of the outer, colored rind from organically grown oranges, grapefruit, tangerines, lemons, or limes and cover them with oil for 1 to 2 weeks, as just described.

Herbal vinegars are easy as pie and keep well as long as you store them properly. Never set them on a sunny windowsill (pretty as that may look). Store vinegars in a cool, dark cupboard and use them up within 3 months. If you want to try your hand at making herbed vinegars, try the simple recipes given here, and then experiment freely. If you aren't too sure about the outcome, make small batches, scaled down to 1 cup vinegar and 2 to 4 tablespoons herbs, then make bigger batches of your successes to give as gifts for family and friends.

Rosemary Vinegar

2 cups fresh rosemary leaves
4 cups cider vinegar

■ Rinse the rosemary, roll lightly with a rolling pin, and then pack into a clean glass jar. Cover with the vinegar, seal the jar, and store in a cool, dark place for 1 to 2 weeks. Shake the jar lightly every day or so. Check the strength after 2 weeks. When the vinegar is infused to your taste, strain it into a clean jar, seal, and refrigerate for up to 3 months.

MAKES ABOUT 3 CUPS

Zippy Herbal Vinegar

1 cup rosemary sprigs, in 6-inch pieces
6 whole sage leaves
2 to 3 whole hot red chiles
1 or 2 whole hot green chiles
3 cloves garlic, peeled
3 to 4 cups cider vinegar

■ Rinse the herbs, roll lightly with a rolling pin, and then place them in a clean quart jar. Add the chiles and garlic and cover with vinegar. Seal the jar tightly and store in a dim cupboard for 2 weeks. Shake the jar lightly every day or so. Check the strength after 2 weeks. When the vinegar is infused to your taste, strain it into a clean jar, seal, and refrigerate for up to 3 months.

MAKES ABOUT 3 CUPS

fall recipes

entrées

Ginger Pork with Pears
Rosemary and Garlic Turkey with Green Peppercorn
  Pan Gravy
Autumn Curried Chicken
Chicken with Blueberries and Hazelnuts
Eggplant and Green Tomato Medallions Parmesan
Summer's End Lasagne

soups and stews

Snappy Snapper Chowder
Hot Tomato Soup
Ratatouille

side dishes

Smoky Eggplant Dip
Zucchini in Basil Oil
Grilled Kale and Broccolini
Yams with Caramelized Onions and Hazelnuts
Walnut, Garlic, and Olive Bread Pudding
Golden Mashed Potatoes with Eggplant
Crispy Sweet Potatoes
Brussels Sprouts in Lemon Herb Sauce

salads

Autumn Harvest Salad
Fall Rice Salad
Wasabi Lime Tuna Salad
Ginger Beet Salad
October Salad
Salad Persephone

baked goods and sweets

Garlic, Sage, and Rosemary Muffins
Basil Corn Muffins with Basil Butter
Peter's Cornbread
Huckleberry Crumble
French Plum Tart
Fall Fruit Crisp
Lactose-Free Pumpkin Pie with Almond-Ginger
  Meringue Topping

'Akane' apple.

fall menus

september

Chicken with Blueberries
and Hazelnuts

Eggplant and Green Tomato
Medallions Parmesan

Autumn Harvest Salad

Huckleberry Crumble

october

Ginger Pork with Pears

Crispy Sweet Potatoes

Zucchini in Basil Oil

October Salad

Fall Fruit Crisp

november

Rosemary and Garlic Turkey with
Green Peppercorn Pan Gravy

Yams with Caramelized Onions
and Hazelnuts

Brussels Sprouts in Lemon Herb Sauce

Lactose-Free Pumpkin Pie with
Almond-Ginger Meringue Topping

entrées

Ginger Pork with Pears

Pears add a juicy sweetness to autumnal dishes like this easy curry dish of firm pears with lean pork, tart dried cranberries, and spicy ginger.

> 2 teaspoons vegetable oil
> 3 or 4 cloves garlic, chopped
> 2- to 3-inch piece ginger root, peeled and chopped
> 4 lean pork steaks, about 1½ pounds total
> 1 white or yellow onion, sliced into ¼-inch rings
> 4 Bartlett or Anjou pears, cored and sliced into wedges
> 2 tablespoons dried cranberries or golden raisins
> ¼ teaspoon kosher or sea salt
> 1 teaspoon garam masala or mild curry powder
> ¾ cup cider vinegar, red wine vinegar, or red wine

■ Preheat the oven to 350°F. Heat the oil in a Dutch oven or heavy, lidded flameproof baking dish over medium-high heat. Add the garlic and ginger and stir-fry until pale golden. Add the pork and sear quickly on both sides, then add the onion and stir-fry until pale golden. Add the pears and cranberries, sprinkle with the salt and garam masala, and stir well. Add the vinegar, cover, and bake for 1 hour.

MAKES 4 SERVINGS

Rosemary and Garlic Turkey with Green Peppercorn Pan Gravy

Gilded, aromatic, and utterly delicious, this simple, classic turkey treatment gets rave reviews from family and friends. The creamy gravy adds the perfect touch of richness, depth, and heat. It is also good made with roast chicken.

> 1 turkey (12 to 20 pounds)
> 1 whole head garlic, cloves peeled and thickly sliced (about 4 slices per clove)

1 cup rosemary sprigs, in 1-inch pieces
4 organic oranges, scrubbed and cut into
    quarters
4 white or yellow onions, peeled and cut
    into quarters
Salt and freshly ground black pepper

Green Peppercorn Pan Gravy

1 tablespoon butter
1 tablespoon flour
¼ teaspoon kosher or sea salt
1 teaspoon drained green peppercorns
About 1½ cups pan juices from the turkey
1 tablespoon dry marsala wine

■ Preheat the oven to 425°F. Rinse the turkey and pat dry. With a sharp boning knife, make 1-inch-deep cuts straight through the skin and flesh all over the outside of the bird, spacing them about 2 inches apart. Put a slice of garlic or a rosemary sprig in each. Fill the turkey cavity with the oranges, onions, remaining garlic slices, and remaining rosemary sprigs.

■ Turn oven temperature down to 350°F, place the turkey breast-side up on a rack in a roasting pan, sprinkle with salt and pepper, and roast until done, about 15 minutes per pound. If desired, baste with the pan juices two or three times each hour; this gives a deep, golden glaze to the skin. When done, cover the bird with foil and let rest 10 minutes before carving.

■ While the turkey is resting, prepare the gravy. In a heavy frying pan, melt the butter over medium-high heat. Add the flour and cook, stirring constantly, until golden brown. Add the salt and peppercorns, then slowly stir in the pan juices until the gravy is the desired consistency. Stir in the marsala and serve with the turkey.

Makes 6+ servings of turkey and 1½ cups of gravy

Autumn Curried Chicken

On a brisk fall evening, this dish warms the spirit as well as the body. Tender chicken breasts cook quickly, so just toss together a green salad, heat some fresh rolls, and call it good.

2 tablespoons virgin olive oil

4 cloves garlic, chopped

4 skinless, boneless chicken breast halves

¼ teaspoon kosher or sea salt

1 teaspoon freshly ground black pepper

1 onion, thinly sliced

1 ripe pear, cored and chopped

1 ripe apple, cored and chopped

1 teaspoon sweet or hot curry powder

¼ teaspoon ground nutmeg

¼ teaspoon ground cumin

¼ teaspoon ground cinnamon

½ cup apple cider

1 bunch cilantro, stemmed, for garnish

■ In a large frying pan, heat the olive oil over medium-high heat. Add the garlic and cook until it is a pale golden color, 2 to 3 minutes. Add the chicken, sprinkling it with the salt and pepper. Cook until browned, 3 to 5 minutes per side, turning once. Add the onion, pear, and apple, stirring to coat with the pan juices. Stir in the curry powder, nutmeg, cumin, and cinnamon, cook for 1 minute, then add the cider.

■ Bring to a simmer, cover, and cook until chicken juices run clear, 10 to 15 minutes. Uncover the pan, increase heat to high, and cook, stirring, until the sauce is reduced by half, 5 to 6 minutes. Serve at once, spooning sauce over each serving and garnishing with the cilantro.

Makes 4 servings

'Liberty' apple.

Chicken with Blueberries and Hazelnuts

The last of the late-cropping blueberries seem to invite savory rather than sweet treatment. The lively bite of garlic and ginger gives this unusual dish a palate-pleasing flavor. The same sauce is lovely served over grilled pork kebabs or fish steaks.

½ cup whole wheat pastry flour
¼ teaspoon kosher or sea salt
½ teaspoon freshly ground black pepper
½ teaspoon fresh lemon thyme or any thyme leaves
½ teaspoon fresh marjoram leaves
1 egg white, lightly beaten
4 skinless, boneless chicken breast halves
½ cup toasted, skinned, chopped hazelnuts, divided
2 teaspoons virgin olive oil
2 cloves garlic, chopped
1-inch piece ginger root, peeled and chopped
1 white or yellow onion, chopped
1 cup blueberries, stemmed

■ Preheat the oven to 350°F. In a wide, shallow dish or pie plate, blend the flour, ⅛ teaspoon each of the salt and pepper, the thyme, and the marjoram.

■ Place the egg white in another wide, shallow dish. Dip the chicken in the egg white and then in the flour mixture to coat. Place in a baking dish, sprinkle with ¼ cup of the hazelnuts, and bake until golden brown, 30 to 40 minutes.

■ In a heavy frying pan, heat the oil and garlic over medium-high heat and cook for 1 minute. Add the ginger and onion, sprinkle with the remaining ⅛ teaspoon salt and ⅜ teaspoon pepper, and cook, stirring, until soft, 3 to 5 minutes.

■ Add the blueberries and bring to a boil. Reduce heat to low, cover, and cook until soft, 2 to 4 minutes. Serve the chicken warm, drizzled with the warm sauce and garnished with the remaining ¼ cup hazelnuts.

MAKES 4 SERVINGS

Eggplant and Green Tomato Medallions Parmesan

For eggplant lovers, this dish will fast become a favorite. Thin slices of vegetables and cheese are dipped in cornmeal and then pan-fried to a crisp, golden finish. For a main dish, serve a plateful with beautiful bread and a big tossed salad embellished with cherry tomatoes and a snappy balsamic vinaigrette. These tidbits also make a savory appetizer or a sumptuous side dish for grilled fish or chicken.

2 eggs, lightly beaten
1 cup finely ground cornmeal
½ teaspoon salt
½ teaspoon freshly ground black pepper
2 tablespoons grated Parmesan cheese
2 to 3 tablespoons virgin olive oil
1 tablespoon butter
1 Japanese eggplant (3 to 4 inches long), cut into ½-inch-thick slices
2 green tomatoes (3 to 4 inches across), cut into 1-inch-thick slices
4 ounces fresh mozzarella cheese, thinly sliced

■ Place a serving platter in the oven and heat the oven to warm. Pour the beaten eggs into a wide, shallow dish; set aside. In a second shallow dish, combine the cornmeal, salt, pepper, and grated cheese.

■ In a heavy frying pan, heat the olive oil and butter over medium-high heat. When butter is foamy, dip the slices of eggplant, green tomato, and mozzarella into the egg mixture, coating both sides, and then into the cornmeal. Fry lightly, 2 to 3 minutes per side. Place the cooked slices on the warm serving platter. Serve hot.

Makes 4 to 6 servings

Summer's End Lasagne

Summer squash, pattypans, and eggplant are layered with noodles, cheeses, and pasta sauce to make an exceptional lasagne at summer's end. This hearty and delicious casserole tastes even better the next day, so make enough for leftovers.

2 tablespoons virgin olive oil
2 cloves garlic, chopped
2 yellow summer squash, sliced
2 pattypan squash, diced
1 eggplant, peeled and diced
1 medium onion. chopped
½ teaspoon salt
½ teaspoon freshly ground black pepper
1 teaspoon fresh oregano leaves
8 ounces lasagna noodles, cooked and
    drained
3 cups garlic and basil pasta sauce
2 cups shredded fresh basil leaves
1 cup grated mozzarella cheese

■ Preheat the oven to 350°F. Lightly coat a 2-quart baking dish with olive oil. In a large frying pan, heat the remaining oil. Add the garlic and cook over medium-high heat until golden, 2 to 3 minutes. Add the squashes, eggplant, and onion, sprinkle with the salt, pepper, and oregano, and cook, stirring, for 1 minute to coat the vegetables with oil.

■ Line the baking dish with a layer of noodles (use one-third of the total) and 1 cup of the pasta sauce. Add half the cooked vegetables and half the basil. Repeat with a second layer of noodles and the remaining vegetables and basil. Top with the remaining noodles and pasta sauce and the mozzarella.

■ Bake until hot through and golden, about 1 hour. Serve hot.

MAKES 6 TO 8 SERVINGS

soups and
stews

Snappy Snapper Chowder

On a gray, drizzly day, this steaming chowder is a heart winner. Chunks of red snapper, 'Yukon Gold' potatoes, and Walla Walla Sweet onions are bathed in a rich vegetable broth that's smoky with chipotle chiles. This recipe works with almost any kind of fish, from salmon to sole, so experiment freely.

1½ pounds unpeeled 'Yukon Gold'
    potatoes, diced
4 cups vegetable broth
¼ teaspoon fresh rosemary leaves
1¼ pounds red snapper fillet, cut into
    1-inch pieces
2 teaspoons virgin olive oil
2 cloves garlic, chopped
1 Walla Walla Sweet onion, chopped
¼ teaspoon kosher or sea salt

1 can (6 to 8 ounces) chipotle peppers in
    adobo sauce
¼ sour cream (nonfat works fine), for
    garnish
4 green onions, thinly sliced, for garnish

■ In a large saucepan, combine the potatoes with the vegetable broth, bring to a boil over high heat, reduce heat to medium, add the rosemary, and simmer until the potatoes are tender, 12 to 15 minutes. Skim off any foam, add the snapper, cover, and reduce the heat to low.

■ In a soup pot, heat the olive oil over medium-high heat, add the garlic, and cook for 1 minute. Add the onion, sprinkle with the salt, and cook, stirring occasionally, until soft, 3 to 5 minutes.

■ Purée the chipotles and add 1 to 2 tablespoons of the purée to the broth (to taste), storing the remainder in the refrigerator for another use. Add the potatoes, fish, and broth to the soup pot, simmer for 5 minutes, and serve, garnished with sour cream and green onions.

MAKES 4 SERVINGS

Fall harvest in Springfield, Oregon.

Hot Tomato Soup

As soon as the evening air turns crisp, it's time to make hot, hearty garden soups again. As the last of the tomatoes ripen on the windowsill, toss a few in the blender with herbs and broth. This delicious, almost-instant soup needs only a quick salad and muffins to round it out.

6 cups fresh tomatoes, diced (with juice)
1 Walla Walla Sweet onion, chopped
1 cup cilantro leaves
1 tablespoon virgin olive oil
2 cloves garlic, chopped
¼ teaspoon kosher or sea salt
¼ teaspoon freshly ground black pepper
1 cup heavy cream (nonfat sour cream works fine)
2 green onions, thinly sliced, for garnish

■ In a blender or food processor, combine the tomatoes, onion, and cilantro and process until fairly smooth; set aside. In a soup pot, heat the olive oil over medium-high heat, add the garlic, and cook, stirring, until golden, 2 to 3 minutes. Add the tomato mixture, salt, and pepper, then reduce heat to medium and heat through. Add the cream and heat through, 2 to 3 minutes; do not boil. Serve hot, garnished with the green onions.

<small>Makes 4 to 6 servings</small>

Ratatouille

In southern France, squash, peppers, and egg-plant are often combined into ratatouille, a glorified vegetable stew. For the fullest flavor, gently simmer the vegetables instead of frying them to mush. The result is so sumptuous that even people who think they don't like eggplant will ask for seconds (just don't tell).

2 tablespoons virgin olive oil
1 white or yellow onion, diced
About ½ teaspoon kosher or sea salt
3 cloves garlic, chopped
1 medium eggplant, unpeeled, diced
   (about 3 cups)
1 red bell pepper, thinly sliced
1 green bell pepper, thinly sliced
2 small zucchini, diced (about 2 cups)

1 yellow summer squash, thinly sliced
   (about 2 cups)
2 to 3 ripe tomatoes, diced (about 2 cups)
About ¼ teaspoon freshly ground black
   pepper
2 tablespoons shredded fresh basil leaves
1 teaspoon fresh oregano leaves

■ In a large pan, heat the oil over medium heat. Add the onion, sprinkle with ¼ teaspoon of the salt, and cook, stirring occasionally, until soft, 3 to 5 minutes. Add the garlic and cook until soft, 2 to 3 minutes. Add the eggplant and peppers, stir to coat with oil, reduce the heat to medium-low, cover, and cook for 10 minutes.

■ Add the zucchini, summer squash, and toma-toes, cover, and cook for another 10 minutes. Season to taste with salt and pepper, add the basil and oregano, reduce the heat to low, and simmer for 10 minutes. Remove the cover and simmer for 5 minutes to reduce the pan juices, if necessary. Serve hot or chilled.

<small>Makes 4 to 6 servings</small>

side dishes

Smoky Eggplant Dip

Most eggplant recipes call for endless oil, so I devised this delicious dip that uses no oil at all. Try it with chips or on vegetables or, best of all, spread it on rye bread and top with smoked salmon, fresh tomatoes, and Walla Walla Sweet onions. Yum! If you don't want to start up the outdoor grill, these will also work under a broiler.

1 large eggplant
2 red bell peppers
½ teaspoon kosher or sea salt
½ teaspoon freshly ground pepper
1 tablespoon lemon juice

■ Start coals in a grill. Prick the eggplant and red peppers with a fork and grill (whole and unpeeled) over medium coals until soft. When cool, peel the eggplant and peppers, seed the peppers, and then chop both coarsely.

■ Purée in a food processor with the salt, pepper, and lemon juice. Serve as a dip.

MAKES 2 CUPS

Zucchini in Basil Oil

This succulent, spicy dish will make the last of your zucchini harvest disappear like magic.

2 tablespoons basil oil (see page 157)
2 cloves garlic, chopped
2 to 3 zucchini (6 inches long), sliced in half lengthwise
½ teaspoon kosher or sea salt
¼ teaspoon freshly ground black pepper
1 to 2 teaspoons balsamic or sherry vinegar

■ In a heavy frying pan, heat the oil over medium-high heat. Add the garlic and cook 1 minute. Add the zucchini, toss to coat with oil, and sprinkle with the salt and pepper. Cover and steam for 1 to 2 minutes, until the zucchini is barely tender. Sprinkle with vinegar to taste and serve at once.

MAKES 4 TO 6 SERVINGS

'Candor' zucchini and 'Pokey Joe' cilantro.

Grilled Kale and Broccolini

If you can't find the slim, spearlike broccolini, use side shoots of regular broccoli or snap off sections of Romanesco broccoli; all taste equally delicious when cooked in this zesty manner.

1 tablespoon olive oil
Juice and grated zest of ½ organic lemon
1 clove garlic, chopped
¼ teaspoon salt
¼ teaspoon freshly ground black pepper
½ teaspoon fresh thyme leaves
1 bunch winter kale, stem ends trimmed
1 pound broccolini, stem ends trimmed

■ Start coals in a grill. In a jar, combine the olive oil, lemon juice and zest, garlic, salt, pepper, and thyme. Shake well, then pour over the vegetables and toss gently.

■ Grill over medium coals for 2 to 3 minutes per side, turning once. Remove to a platter, cover with foil, and let sit for 5 minutes before serving.

Makes 4 to 6 servings

Yams with Caramelized Onions and Hazelnuts

As a side dish, try this voluptuous combination of baked yams with caramelized onions and hazelnuts (it also works well with sweet potatoes). This dish tastes so rich and satisfying you might not even need dessert.

4 medium yams, such as 'Red Jewel',
    peeled and cut into quarters
6 teaspoons virgin olive oil
About ¾ teaspoon kosher or any salt
1 teaspoon freshly ground black pepper
2 onions, cut in half and thinly sliced
¼ teaspoon sugar
1 cup toasted, skinned, chopped hazelnuts

■ Preheat the oven to 350°F. Rub the yams with 1 teaspoon of the olive oil and arrange them in a baking dish. Sprinkle with the salt and ½ teaspoon of the pepper and bake until tender, 30 to 45 minutes.

■ Heat the remaining oil in a frying pan over medium-high heat. Add the onions, sprinkle with salt to taste (start with ¼ teaspoon), the remaining ½ teaspoon pepper, and the sugar. Cook, stirring often, until the onions turn pale golden. Reduce heat to low and continue to cook slowly, stirring occasionally, until onions are dark golden brown, about 15 minutes.

Top the yams with the onions and sprinkle with the hazelnuts. Return to the oven for 10 minutes, then serve at once.

MAKES 4 TO 6 SERVINGS

Walnut, Garlic, and Olive Bread Pudding

This is the perfect side dish for pork, chicken, or salmon, especially when made with crusty olive bread. Day-old bread becomes moist and savory in this easy dish—which tastes even better the next day.

4 cups (about 1 loaf) olive bread, cut into
    ½-inch cubes
4 cups milk or vegetable broth
2 tablespoons butter

2 tablespoons virgin olive oil or walnut oil
3 cloves garlic, chopped
1 onion, chopped
¼ teaspoon fresh thyme leaves
½ teaspoon dried marjoram, crushed
1 teaspoon fresh rosemary leaves
¼ teaspoon kosher or sea salt
½ teaspoon freshly ground black pepper
1 cup chopped walnuts
½ cup grated Romano or Parmesan cheese

■ Preheat the oven to 350°F. Put the bread cubes in a baking dish (2 quarts or larger). Heat the milk in a medium saucepan, then drizzle over the bread and let stand for 15 minutes.

■ In a saucepan, melt the butter with the oil over medium heat. Add the garlic and onion and cook until pale golden, 2 to 3 minutes. Add the thyme, marjoram, rosemary, salt, and pepper and cook, stirring, for 2 minutes, then pour over the bread mixture. Sprinkle with the walnuts and cheese and bake until puffed and golden, about 1 hour.

Makes 6 to 8 servings

Golden Mashed Potatoes with Eggplant

If you want an outstanding side dish, try a fluffy, golden mound of 'Yukon Gold' potatoes mashed with oven-roasted eggplant. It may sound odd,

Eggplants need warm soil to grow well.

but this meltingly luscious dish is a universal favorite every time I make it.

1 medium eggplant
1 pound 'Yukon Gold' potatoes, peeled and quartered
About ½ teaspoon salt
2 cloves garlic, chopped
1½ to 2½ teaspoons olive oil
½ teaspoon fresh oregano leaves

■ Preheat the oven to 425°F. Rub a baking dish with a bit of olive oil. Slice the eggplant in half lengthwise and place in the dish, cut side down. Bake until soft, about 45 minutes. Set aside.

■ Place the potatoes in a medium saucepan and add water to cover. Add ¼ teaspoon of the salt and half of the garlic, bring to a boil over high heat, then reduce the heat to medium and simmer until tender, 12 to 14 minutes. Drain and mash with olive oil to taste, the remaining garlic, and the oregano. Scrape the eggplant pulp from the skin and mash with the potatoes, adding salt to taste.

<small>Makes 4 to 6 servings</small>

Crispy Sweet Potatoes

Light and crunchy on the outside, creamy and soft inside, this irresistible side dish provides a lovely change of pace and is less densely caloric than regular old mashed potatoes.

2 tablespoons virgin olive oil
2 shallots, minced
Juice and grated zest of ½ organic lemon
4 sweet potatoes, peeled
½ teaspoon kosher or sea salt
½ teaspoon Aleppo pepper or ground black pepper

■ Preheat the oven to 400°F. In a large bowl or a resealable plastic bag, combine the olive oil, shallots, lemon juice and zest, set aside. Cut the sweet potatoes in half lengthwise, then cut into 2-inch chunks. Toss in the oil mixture to coat, then arrange in a single layer on a baking sheet, drizzling any extra oil over them. Sprinkle with the salt and pepper and bake until crisp, turning twice, about 20 minutes per side. Serve warm.

<small>Makes 8 servings</small>

Brussels Sprouts in Lemon Herb Sauce

Peppery Brussels sprouts are improved by a touch of frost and can be added to soups and stews or served alone. I especially like them with this lively herb sauce, which also does wonders for cauliflower and carrots.

2 cups Brussels sprouts, cut in half lengthwise
1 tablespoon olive oil
3 cloves garlic, finely chopped
Juice and grated zest of 1 organic lemon
About ¼ teaspoon kosher or sea salt
About ¼ teaspoon freshly ground black pepper
2 tablespoons shredded fresh lemon balm leaves
1 teaspoon fresh lemon thyme leaves
1 teaspoon cornstarch

■ Put the Brussels sprouts in a steamer basket in a large saucepan over an inch of water and steam until tender, 6 to 8 minutes. While they cook, heat the oil in a medium saucepan over medium-high heat. Add the garlic and 1 teaspoon of the lemon zest and sizzle until pale golden, 2 to 3 minutes. Drain the Brussels sprouts and add to the pan, stirring to coat them with oil. Sprinkle with salt and pepper to taste. Add the lemon balm, lemon thyme, and lemon juice to taste, a teaspoon at a time. Add water to make about ⅓ cup liquid.

■ In a small bowl, dissolve the cornstarch into 1 tablespoon cold water. Slowly stir into the sauce, stirring constantly, cooking until sauce is thick and clear, about 2 minutes. Serve at once, garnished with the remaining grated lemon zest.

Makes 4 servings

salads

Autumn Harvest Salad

Enliven a tossed salad of garden greens and late vegetables with lemon and garlic, adding a handful of blueberries or huckleberries for zip and hazelnuts for crunch. Marinate ripe avocado slices in the dressing for a delicious crowning touch.

1 ripe avocado, sliced
¼ cup virgin olive oil
Juice and grated zest of 1 organic lemon
2 cloves garlic, minced or pressed
¼ teaspoon kosher or sea salt
¼ teaspoon freshly ground black pepper
½ teaspoon sugar
6 cups fresh greens
1 red bell pepper, thinly sliced
½ cup thinly sliced zucchini
½ Walla Walla Sweet onion, chopped
1 cup cilantro leaves
½ cup blueberries or huckleberries
¼ cup toasted, skinned, chopped hazelnuts, for garnish

■ Arrange the avocado slices in a shallow bowl. In a jar, combine the olive oil, lemon juice and zest, garlic, salt, pepper, and sugar. Shake well, and pour over the avocado slices.

■ In a salad bowl, arrange the greens. Top with the red pepper, zucchini, onion, cilantro, and blueberries. Arrange the avocado slices over the salad, drizzle with the dressing, and serve, garnished with hazelnuts.

MAKES 4 SERVINGS

Fall Rice Salad

Whatever the fall garden offers can be used in this hearty salad, which makes a rib-sticking side dish for grilled fish or chicken. It also works great as an entrée.

1 cup brown or jasmine rice
1 tablespoon olive oil
2 cloves garlic, mashed

2 small yellow pattypan or summer squash, thinly sliced

2 small zucchini, chopped

1 cup sliced green beans (½-inch pieces)

1 cup sweet corn kernels

1 Walla Walla Sweet or any sweet onion, chopped

½ teaspoon kosher or sea salt

1 teaspoon minced fresh lemon thyme or any thyme

4 sprigs lemon balm, minced

4 sprigs silver mint (or any mint), minced

4 ripe tomatoes, diced (juice reserved)

1 teaspoon drained capers

¼ teaspoon freshly ground black pepper

½ to 1 cup sour cream (nonfat works fine), for garnish

■ Cook the rice according to the package directions. In a frying pan, heat the oil over medium heat. Add the garlic, brown on all sides to flavor the oil, and discard. Add the squash, zucchini, green beans, corn, and onions, stir to coat with oil, and cook until soft, 3 to 5 minutes. Sprinkle with the salt, add the herbs, and cook for 30

Fall harvest of kale, tomatoes, peppers, carrots, chard, acorn squash, and more.

seconds to bloom the flavor. Stir in the tomatoes with their juice and the capers. Fold the vegetable mixture into the hot rice. Serve warm, topped with freshly ground black pepper and garnished with sour cream.

Makes 4 servings

Farmers market bounty.

Wasabi Lime Tuna Salad

To celebrate summer's end with panache, make this lively Pan-Asian version of the classic niçoise tuna and vegetable salad. If your store doesn't carry wasabi lime mayonnaise, whip up the quick homemade version offered here. It also makes a great dip for raw vegetables and adds snap to grilled salmon.

1½ pounds tuna fillet
1 teaspoon vegetable oil
2 cloves garlic, minced
¼ teaspoon kosher or sea salt
¼ teaspoon freshly ground black pepper
1 cup Wasabi Lime Mayonnaise, store-
    bought or homemade
1 teaspoon drained capers
6 cups fresh greens
2 stalks celery, thinly sliced
2 ripe tomatoes, cut into wedges
1 red bell pepper, thinly sliced
½ Walla Walla Sweet onion, chopped
1 cup flat Italian parsley leaves
4 hard-boiled eggs, cut into wedges

1 lime, cut into quarters
¼ cup niçoise olives, drained

Wasabi Lime Mayonnaise

    1 cup mayonnaise (nonfat works fine)
    Juice and grated zest of 1 organic lime
    1 clove garlic, minced
    ¼ teaspoon kosher or sea salt
    ¼ teaspoon freshly ground black pepper
    1 to 2 teaspoons wasabi paste

■ To make the Wasabi Lime Mayonnaise, stir each ingredient into mayonnaise slowly, adding lime juice and wasabi to taste (begin with 1 teaspoon of the wasabi). Refrigerate leftovers for up to 3 days.

■ Start coals in a grill or preheat the broiler. Rinse the fish, rub with the oil, then pat the garlic and ⅛ teaspoon each of the salt and pepper on both sides. Grill or broil until barely opaque, 2 to 3 minutes per side, turning once. In a medium bowl, blend the Wasabi Lime Mayonnaise and capers; set aside.

■ Divide the greens among 4 dinner plates. Gently toss the celery, tomatoes, red pepper, onion, and parsley with the mayonnaise, then arrange on the greens. Cut the tuna into 4 pieces, and top each plate with a piece of tuna, some hard-boiled egg, and a lime wedge for the fish. Serve with a dish of olives.

<small>MAKES 4 SERVINGS OF SALAD AND 1 CUP MAYONNAISE</small>

Organic brown and green Araucana chicken eggs.

Ginger Beet Salad

Julienned (matchstick-cut) vegetables make this salad especially attractive, though dicing works fine too. Apple chunks and sweet orange juice offset the tangy ginger, as do salty toasted cashews. Serve this with grilled salmon or chicken to give a plain meal a lift.

> 3 cooked beets, peeled and julienned (or diced), about 3 cups
> 2 carrots, julienned (or thinly sliced), about 1½ cups
> 2 stalks celery, thinly sliced
> 1 unpeeled organic apple, cored and diced
> ¼ cup cashews, toasted, for garnish

Dressing

> ⅓ cup rice vinegar
> ½-inch piece ginger root, peeled and finely chopped
> 1 clove garlic, minced
> Juice and grated zest of 1 organic orange

■ To prepare the dressing, in a food processor or blender combine the vinegar, ginger root, garlic, orange juice and zest. Purée to blend, and set aside.

■ In a serving bowl, gently toss the beets, carrots, celery, and apple with the ginger dressing. Serve garnished with cashews.

Makes 4 to 6 servings

October Salad

Try this crunchy, piquant salad for a change from the usual. Dress it with raspberry vinaigrette or your favorite citrus dressing.

> 2 cups shredded bok choy
> 2 cups shredded sweet kale
> 1 cup flat Italian parsley leaves
> 1 cup cilantro leaves
> 1 unpeeled organic pear, cored and diced
> 1 unpeeled organic apple, cored and diced
> ½ sweet red onion, chopped
> 2 tablespoons dried cranberries
> ½ cup raspberry vinaigrette or any citrus dressing

■ In a salad bowl, gently toss together the bok choy, kale, parsley, and cilantro. Top with the pear, apple, onion, and cranberries, drizzle with the dressing, toss lightly, and serve at once.

<small>MAKES 4 TO 6 SERVINGS</small>

Salad Persephone

This hearty, warm salad combines Earth Mother root vegetables and fresh greens. Pan-roasted beets, 'Lady Finger' potatoes, and carrots are tossed in an orange juice dressing with finely shredded spinach and kale and topped with a sparkler of pomegranate seeds.

¼ cup virgin olive oil
2 cloves garlic, pressed or minced
1 teaspoon fresh rosemary leaves
2 medium beets, peeled and cut in half lengthwise
1 pound 'Lady Finger' potatoes, peeled and cut in half lengthwise
2 medium carrots, peeled and cut in half lengthwise
½ teaspoon kosher or sea salt
½ teaspoon freshly ground black pepper
1 bunch spinach, stemmed and shredded
1 bunch 'Black Dragon' kale, stemmed and shredded
1 cup flat Italian parsley leaves
Juice of 1 organic orange
1 large pomegranate, seeded (see page 184)

■ Preheat the oven to 400°F. In a bowl, combine the olive oil, garlic, and rosemary and stir well. Rub the beets, potatoes, and carrots with the oil, then arrange, cut sides down, in a baking dish. Sprinkle with ¼ teaspoon each of the salt and pepper and bake until fork-tender, about 30 minutes. Slice thinly.

■ In a salad bowl, toss the spinach, kale, and parsley together and top with the vegetables. Add the orange juice to the remaining oil mixture, drizzle over the salad, and serve, garnished with pomegranate seeds.

<small>MAKES 4 TO 6 SERVINGS</small>

cook's tip

look pomegranates over carefully, avoiding any with soft or mushy spots. The rind should be firm and a bit leathery, but not brittle or dry. Choose the heaviest fruit you can find and use them right away for best flavor. Seeding pomegranates can be an adventure; wear a large apron and an old shirt to minimize the rich red stains from the juicy little seed capsules. Scatter the glowing little seeds over fruit or green salads, use them to garnish grilled fish or fowl, or toss them with a light vinaigrette for a tart accent. Pomegranate seeds are also lovely on sorbet.

baked goods and sweets

Garlic, Sage, and Rosemary Muffins

These savory golden muffins make an outstanding accompaniment for roast pork, baked chicken, or grilled salmon. Add a tossed salad with a citrusy dressing and revel in the harmonic flavors.

1 tablespoon virgin olive oil
3 cloves garlic, chopped
1 Walla Walla Sweet onion, finely chopped
¾ teaspoon salt
4 leaves fresh sage, shredded
2 teaspoons fresh rosemary leaves
½ teaspoon drained green peppercorns
1 cup all-purpose flour
½ cup whole wheat pastry flour
1 tablespoon baking powder

½ cup quick-cooking rolled oats
1 large egg, beaten until blended
1 cup buttermilk or milk
3 tablespoons vegetable oil

■ Preheat the oven to 400°F. Line 12 muffin cups with paper liners. In a small saucepan, heat the olive oil over medium-high heat. Add the garlic and onion, sprinkle with ¼ teaspoon of the salt, and cook, stirring, until soft, 2 to 3 minutes. Add the sage, rosemary, and green peppercorns and cook for 1 minute, then remove from the heat.

■ In a mixing bowl, sift together the flours, the remaining ½ teaspoon salt, and baking powder. Stir in the oats. Add the egg and milk, stir well, and then stir in the vegetable oil and the onion mixture. Stir to combine, and spoon into the muffin cups. Bake until golden brown, 20 to 25 minutes. Cool in the pan for 5 minutes before serving.

Makes 12 large muffins

Basil Corn Muffins

Simple soups taste super when served with these hot muffins, juicy with corn and spicy with fresh basil. Serve them warm or split, toasted, and slathered with fresh Basil Butter.

1½ cups yellow cornmeal
½ cup unbleached white flour
1 tablespoon baking powder
½ teaspoon salt
1 cup sour cream or yogurt (nonfat works fine)
2 tablespoons virgin olive oil
1 teaspoon drained green peppercorns
1 cup corn kernels, thawed if frozen
1 cup shredded fresh basil leaves

Basil Butter

¼ cup (½ stick) unsalted butter, at room temperature
½ cup shredded fresh basil leaves
1 teaspoon chopped fresh lemon thyme leaves

■ To prepare the Basil Butter, combine all of the ingredients in a food processor or blender and process to a smooth paste. Spoon into a small bowl and chill until firm. Store in the refrigerator for up to 3 days.

■ Preheat the oven to 350°F. Line 12 muffin cups with paper liners. In a medium bowl, sift together the cornmeal, flour, baking powder, and salt; set aside.

■ In a mixing bowl, combine the sour cream, olive oil, peppercorns, corn, and basil. Quickly stir in the dry ingredients and then spoon the batter into the muffin cups. Bake until golden, 25 to 30 minutes. Serve warm.

Makes about 12 muffins and ½ cup of Basil Butter

Peter's Cornbread

My son Peter's favorite cornbread recipe takes just a few minutes to assemble and cooks while you fix the soup or reheat the stew. Just a bit of bubbling hot butter gives this golden bread a sumptuously crispy crust that doesn't need any more butter spread on top. Add a fresh green salad and you have a delicious meal that satisfies body and spirit.

3 tablespoons vegetable oil
1 tablespoon butter
1 cup cornmeal (freshly ground is best)
½ cup unbleached white flour
½ cup whole wheat pastry flour
1 tablespoon sugar
1 tablespoon baking powder
½ teaspoon salt
1½ cups buttermilk
1 egg, beaten
2 tablespoons grated hard cheese, such as pecorino or Romano

■ Put 1 tablespoon of the oil and the butter in a 9-inch cast-iron frying pan and place the pan in the oven. Preheat oven to 425°F. Sift the cornmeal, flours, sugar, baking powder, and salt into a medium bowl; set aside.

■ In a large bowl, combine the buttermilk, egg, and remaining 2 tablespoons vegetable oil. Stir in the dry ingredients, then pour into the hot pan. Sprinkle with the cheese and bake until firm and golden brown, about 20 minutes. Cut into wedges and serve at once.

Serves at least one

Huckleberry Crumble

This rich, tender dessert also tastes fabulous made with fresh blackberries or marionberries. A hint of nutmeg gives spice to the fruit, while lemon zest makes the buttery topping memorable.

> 4 cups huckleberries
> 1 to 2 tablespoons fructose or sugar
> Juice and grated zest of 1 organic lemon
> ⅛ teaspoon ground nutmeg
> ½ cup (1 stick) butter, at room temperature
> ½ cup whole wheat pastry flour
> ½ cup unbleached white flour
> 1 teaspoon baking powder
> ¼ cup brown sugar

■ Preheat the oven to 350°F. Spread the berries in a deep pie dish and sprinkle with the fructose or sugar, lemon juice, and nutmeg; set aside.

■ In a small bowl, cut the butter into the flour well, then blend in the baking powder, lemon zest, and brown sugar. Gently spread the crumble topping over the fruit, but don't pat it down.

■ Bake until pale golden, about 25 minutes. Serve warm.

MAKES 6 TO 8 SERVINGS

French Plum Tart

Glazed and glorious, this elegant tart tastes splendid made with any fruit, from raspberries and peaches (glaze them with raspberry or peach jam and lime juice) to blackberries and apples.

½ cup (1 stick) butter, at room temperature
3 tablespoons sugar
⅛ teaspoon salt
1 cup whole wheat pastry flour
1 egg, lightly beaten
2 cups halved pitted plums
2 tablespoons plum jam
Juice and grated zest of 1 organic orange

■ Preheat the oven to 350°F. In a medium bowl, cream the butter with the sugar and salt, then work in the flour with your fingers or a fork. Gently stir in the egg. On a floured surface, roll the dough out gently to a 8- to 9-inch circle and slip it into a shallow 8-inch tart or pie pan. Bake until pale golden, 10 to 12 minutes. Cool.

■ Arrange the plum halves, cut sides down, in a single layer in the tart shell. Heat the plum jam with the orange juice and zest over medium heat until jam is melted, and pour over the plums. Bake until heated through, 20 to 25 minutes. Serve warm or cold.

MAKES 6 SERVINGS

cook's tip

Late summer/early fall brings a heavy harvest of fruit to the market, including a plethora of plums. For tarts and simple flans, the best-flavored plums are the Italian prune plums, which keep their tart-sweet balance longer than plumper types. For baking, look for firm fruit that still has an intact stem end (no tears). For fruit salad, pick chubby, tender Santa Rosa plums or the delicately flavored Mirabelles and Greengages, which also work well with fish or chicken (use them as you would use green grapes).

Fall Fruit Crisp

This wheat-free crisp is a seasonal favorite at our house. Try blending apples and pears or any late fruit, from blueberries and raspberries to peaches.

6 cups sliced fruit (apples/pears,
    blackberries/apples, peaches/
    raspberries, etc.)
½ cup fructose or sugar
½ cup rice flour
½ cup barley flour
½ teaspoon ground nutmeg or coriander
¼ cup (½ stick) butter, at room
    temperature
½ cup lightly packed brown sugar
1 pint vanilla ice cream

■ Preheat the oven to 350°F. Layer the fruit in a 2-quart baking dish, sprinkle with the fructose or sugar, and set aside. In a small bowl, sift together the flours and the nutmeg; set aside. In a medium bowl, cream together the butter and brown sugar, then blend in the flour mixture (the mixture will be crumbly). Crumble evenly over the fruit and bake until golden brown, about 1 hour. Serve warm with vanilla ice cream.

MAKES 4 TO 6 SERVINGS

Lactose-Free Pumpkin Pie with Almond-Ginger Meringue Topping

The search for the perfect pumpkin pie is ongoing for my family, with many variations on the traditional theme. This healthy, refreshing version features coriander and fresh orange juice with an airy meringue topping.

  1½ cups cooked pumpkin purée (canned works fine)

  ½ cup fructose, or ⅔ cup brown sugar

  1 teaspoon ground coriander

  1 teaspoon ground ginger

  ¼ teaspoon ground nutmeg

  ¼ teaspoon salt

  Juice and grated zest of 2 organic oranges

  2 eggs, lightly beaten

  1 cup nonfat vanilla soymilk or milk

  1 unbaked 9-inch pie crust

Almond-Ginger Meringue

  2 egg whites

  ¼ cup granulated sugar

  Few grains salt

  ¼ teaspoon vanilla extract

  ⅓ cup finely chopped crystallized ginger

  ¼ cup finely chopped toasted almonds

■ Preheat the oven to 450°F. In a mixing bowl, combine the pumpkin, fructose, spices, and salt until the fructose is dissolved. Stir in the orange juice, zest, eggs, and milk. Pour into the pie shell and bake for 15 minutes. Lower the heat to 350° and bake until the filling is set, 40 to 50 minutes.

■ While the pie is baking, prepare the Almond-Ginger Meringue: Using an electric mixer, beat the egg whites to the soft peak stage. Slowly add the sugar while continuing to beat. Fold in the salt and vanilla, then add the ginger and almonds. When the pie comes out of the oven, turn the heat to 425°F and allow to preheat for a few minutes. Spread the meringue over the baked pie, covering the surface completely. Bake until the meringue is golden brown, 3 to 5 minutes.

MAKES 6 TO 8 SERVINGS

Fall garden with lumina pumpkin.

fall gardening calendar

what to plant	Berries (all kinds), broccoli, broccolini, fruit trees (all kinds), garlic, hardy herbs, kale, leeks, lettuce, mustard greens, onions, peas, shallots, spinach, Swiss chard
what to harvest	Apples, berries, Brussels sprouts, carrots, dried shell beans, eggplant, melons, parsnips, peppers, potatoes, pumpkins, squash, tomatoes, zucchini
what's in the market	Apples, figs, hazelnuts, parsnips, pears, plums, potatoes, turnips, winter squash

gardening notes for fall ingredients

■ *Apples* The maritime Northwest isn't really prime apple country, but even a small yard can hold a tiny orchard of dwarf trees that will easily produce enough fruit for a small family. Look for low-grafted trees that have multiple grafts, each with a different kind of apple. These four- and five-way trees are grafted with compatible pollinators (many apple varieties need companions in order to set fruit well), so you'll get several kinds of apples from one small tree. Some of the extra-dwarf trees can be grown in a whisky barrel.

'Akane' apple.

Apples need full sun and are best placed on sloping ground where frost can roll away. Mounded beds suit them well, as does deep compost mulch and regular feeding with an organic fertilizer. Even moisture is important through the growing season so the apples can develop and fill out properly. Underplant apples with herbs and spring-blooming flowers to encourage bees to visit often in spring, when the flowers need pollination in order to set fruit.

■ *Broccolini* Also called broccoli raab, broccolini looks something like a cross between asparagus and broccoli side shoots. This tender-crisp vegetable has a delicate, earthy flavor that is brought out by grilling or steaming. Grow broccoli raab in mounded beds amended and mulched with compost.

Sown under cover, spring crops can be started as early as February and March. Sow again in June and July for summer and fall crops, feeding with organic fertilizers rather than high-nitrogen feeds for best flavor. In a mild fall, you can often get an extra crop in by sowing seed in September and early October.

Territorial Seed Company usually offers at least a couple of types of broccolini, including the very tender 'Sorrento' and the spiky 'Zamboni', which is commonly grown in Italy.

■ *Brussels Sprouts* Home-grown Brussels sprouts have the decided advantage of being picked when you choose to harvest them, not for marketing convenience. Early sprouts can be bitter and very peppery. Wait until a few frosts have occurred and you'll find that a marvelous sweetness develops in the flavor.

Brussels sprouts do best in deep, mounded beds of loamy soil amended with plenty of compost to help neutralize acid clay or sand. Sow the seed from mid-May through June, choosing a few early croppers like 'Bubbles' as well as later varieties like 'Vancouver'. My favorite is a beautiful dark red Italian form called 'Rubine', which needs early sowing to come to term properly.

Brussels sprouts do best when fed organic, slow fertilizers rather than high-nitrogen feeds. Give them alfalfa meal, kelp, and some soy or cottonseed meal in early summer, then add alfalfa again in early fall. Keep them evenly moist but never soggy, and mulch young plants with compost. As the sprouts fill out, trim away the lower leaves as close to the stem as you can manage. Harvest the largest sprouts from the bottom of the stalks first, leaving the smaller, upper ones to fill out before picking them.

■ *Eggplant* Tropical heat lovers, eggplants need warm soil (at least 60°F) to grow well. Set out young plants after all frosts are past (usually after Memorial Day) in mounded soil in full sun. Protect young plants with floating row cover, waxed paper hot-caps, or water-filled devices like Wall-O-Waters. Feed them moderately with organic fertilizer and composted manure and keep them evenly moist so they never stop growing. Interplant with herbs and annual flowers to bring in the bees for best pollination.

■ *Huckleberries* Whether evergreen or deciduous, blue-black or red, our native huckleberries are extraordinarily delicious, with the tart-sweet tingle shared by red currants and European gooseberries. If you have native plants in the garden, give them compost instead of fertilizer and keep them well away from any irrigation systems; native plants can be killed with kindness. Grow nursery-bought huckleberries like blueberries (see page 142), but give them afternoon shade.

■ *Peppers* Heat-loving peppers take a while to ripen in cool maritime summers, and we can harvest them well into September and even in October. Start peppers indoors or buy young plants and set them out after Memorial Day, when the soil is at least 60°F. Grow peppers in greenhouses or in mounded beds in full sun, and enrich the soil with plenty of compost.

Protect young pepper plants with Wall-O-Waters or floating row cover to help them adjust to our cool nights. Feed them regularly with organic fertilizers and kelp, and provide enough moisture to keep them growing well (if slowly), but never let them get soggy.

Yellow bell peppers will turn orange and then red as they ripen; harvest them at any stage you prefer. All peppers, but especially green bell peppers, can taste bitter if fed too much artificial fertilizer. Compost helps bring out the flavors in all peppers, both sweet and snappy.

■ *Pumpkins* Pumpkins are prima donna crops, requiring lots of everything, from space to food and water. Plant in spring after the last frost date. They grow well in mounded beds in full sun, and do best when given transplant fertilizer at planting time and then fed every few weeks with a mild (5-5-5) all-purpose feed. Keep the soil moist with drip irrigation or leaky hose lines under the mulch; avoid wetting the foliage, which can trigger molds and mildews. Since incomplete pollination results in really weird-looking pumpkins, use a cover crop of sweet alyssum and other simple flowers to keep the bees visiting.

■ *Zucchini* The perfect first crop for a beginning gardener, zucchini grows happily in mounded beds in full sun. Plant after Memorial Day, when the ground is warm. Give them plenty of room and water the roots, not the plants; keep the foliage dry to avoid disease. Feed moderately and maintain even moisture so the vegetables fill out properly. If zucchini start to form but then start rotting before they fill out completely, they were not fully pollinated. Interplant with sweet alyssum and hardy annuals to bring in the bees (it takes many visits to fully pollinate many vegetables).

My favorite zucchini is 'Black Beauty', a firm, tender straight squash with lovely flavor. I also grow 'Gold Bush', a yellow zucchini with exceptional eating quality, as well as yellow crookneck and golden 'Sunburst' pattypan summer squash. If any of these doesn't fruit properly, surround the plant with sweet alyssum, which will bring in the bees and ensure a good crop.

Acorn squash, 'Baby Bear' pumpkin, and 'Chocolate' snakeroot.

index

a – c

acorn squash
    gardening notes, 40–41
    Savory Acorn Squash, 23
Almond Ginger Meringue, 191
alyssum, 2–3
aphids, 104–5
apples
    in Fall Fruit Crisp, 189
    in French Winter Beet Salad, 32–33
    gardening notes, 192–93
    in October Salad, 182–83
arugula
    Arugula Salad with Cherry-Chive Vinaigrette, 82–83
    gardening notes, 145
asparagus
    Asparagus Salad with Creamy Herb Dressing, 85
    Asparagus with Shallot, Thyme, Parsley, and Lemon Sauce, 73–74
    gardening notes, 90–91
avocado
    in Autumn Harvest Salad, 178
    in Chilled Green Goddess Soup, 72
    Cucumber and Avocado Soup, 118
    in Winter Salad Supreme, 31
basil
    Basil Butter, 185–86
    Basil Corn Muffins, 185–86
    Basil Dressing, 129–30

Basil Oil, 157
    gardening notes, 140–41
    Grilled Salmon with Lavender and Basil, 114–15
    puréed, freezing, 121
    in Summer's End Lasagne, 167
    in Winter Salad Supreme, 31
    Zucchini in Basil Oil, 172
beans
    in Fall Rice Salad, 178–79
    gardening notes, 141
    in Insalata di Fagioli e Tonno (Italian Tuna Salad), 128
beds, laying out, 154
bees, attracting, 2–3
beets
    Beet and Orange Salsa, 12
    French Winter Beet Salad, 32–33
    gardening notes, 41
    Ginger Beet Salad, 182
    in Salad Persephone, 183
bell jars, 4
berries
    in Autumn Harvest Salad, 178
    in Fall Fruit Crisp, 189
    gardening notes, 99, 142–43, 148–49
    in Summer Garden Shake, 139
    See also individual entries
beverages
    Lavender Lemonade, 115
    Summer Garden Shake, 139
blackberries
    in Fall Fruit Crisp, 189
    gardening notes, 142
blood oranges
    Rhubarb and Blood Orange Chutney, 61
blueberries
    in Autumn Harvest Salad, 178

Chicken with Blueberries and Hazelnuts, 165
    gardening notes, 142–43
    Pork Medallions with Blueberries and Ginger, 110
    Raspberry-Blueberry Rollups, 136
    in Red, White, and Blueberry Salad with Fireworks Dressing, 131
bok choy
    in Asparagus Salad with Creamy Herb Dressing, 85
    in Crisp Chicken Salad with Chipotle Cream Dressing, 126–27
    in Fresh Corn Salad with Sweet Chili-Lime Dressing, 130
    gardening notes, 41–43, 145
    in October Salad, 182–83
    in Satsuma Salad, 28
    in Snow Pea Salad, 83
    in Stir-Fried Asian Greens and Pea Vines, 122–23
    in Winter Salad Supreme, 31
boysenberries
    gardening notes, 142
bread
    Peter's Cornbread, 186
    Rosemary Bread, 35
bread pudding
    Hazelnut-Cranberry Bread Pudding, 33–34
    bread pudding, Walnut, Garlic, and Olive Bread Pudding, 174–75
broccoli
    about, 76
    Broccoli with Creamy Sorrel Sauce, 76–77
    gardening notes, 91–92

special thanks

to the following gardeners whose gardens and produce are featured in this book:

Leann Olson, Coos Bay, OR
Sherold Barr and John Kaib, Eugene, OR
Tom & Mary Jo Ten Pas, Philomath, OR
Everett & Mary Yearous, Eugene, OR
Debra Martin & Bill Booth, Horton Road Organics, Blachly, OR
Herrick Farms, Springfield, OR
Julie O'Donald, Brier, WA
Mel & H.J. Lindley, Eugene, OR
Fairie Perennial and Herb Garden, Tumwater, WA
Bellevue Botanical Garden, Bellevue, WA
Winter Green Farm, Noti, OR
Doe Tabor, Eugene, OR
Kuenz Berry Farm, Eugene, OR
Log House Plants, Cottage Grove, OR
Lindsay Reaves, Waterville, OR
Mrs. Mullen garden/Pamela and Paul Panum design, Harrisburg, OR
Max and Don Hazen, Everett, WA
Christy Nordstrom, Seattle, WA
Forever Lavender Farm, Cottage Grove, OR

about the author

Ann Lovejoy loves to cook (and eat!) almost as much as she loves to garden. Her columns on cooking and gardening run each week in the *Seattle Post-Intelligencer* and her articles appear in numerous national magazines. Author of more than twenty gardening books and winner of many awards, Ann is a popular national lecturer on sustainable design and related topics. She lives on Bainbridge Island, Washington. This is her second cookbook.

about the photographer

Robin Bachtler Cushman is a horticultural and garden photographer based in Eugene, Oregon. Her work has appeared in *Sunset*, *Horticulture*, and *Fine Gardening* magazines, as well as many books and newspapers.